Letters to Pastors

—⁓⁓—

By Ron Walters

Letters to Pastors
by Ron Walters

Printed in the United States of America

ISBN 978-1-60647-344-3

www.xulonpress.com

Contents

—⟐—

Introduction

—ɱ—

Some years ago *USA Today* published a list of *The Least Stressful Jobs in America*. Pastoring was #1 on the list. Obviously the writer wasn't a pastor, hadn't watched a pastor work, and possibly didn't even know a pastor.

Pastoring is an anomaly. For those of us who've heard that unmistakable call from God, it became an offer we couldn't refuse. It fit with our DNA. It's what sounds the trumpets each morning. And, if done properly, it's the single most difficult job we've ever known.

Pastoring? Stressless? I don't think so!

When Susan and I moved to San Francisco in 1994, I took on the managerial role of KFAX, a Christian formatted radio station in America's 4th largest market. San Francisco, as you know, is not the Bible belt. In fact, it's not even the Bible suspenders. And yet day-in-and-day-out faithful men of God serve the churches of that region with honor and distinction. Very few will ever gain public notoriety, even fewer will have large congregations.

Having pastored for many years, I felt as much akin to these pastors as I did with my radio cronies. I knew their plight. Therefore each month I wrote a letter of encouragement to the few pastors I knew—about 25 in the beginning. The letters were meant to lift them up, to give and never ask for anything. And, if I could, provide "stealable" material, because pastors are forever in research mode.

Therefore, each Pastors Letter was filled with creative ideas, stories, and helpful data that would first encourage them, but also make their assignment easier.

And it seemed to work. The original list of 25 pastors grew to 50, then 100, then 1,000. Currently 50,000 pastors all over the country are receiving these letters.

Many have written to say thanks. Some are from large, even mega churches. But most are from medium to small churches, guys with the least amount of time for study, research and sermon prep. To all, the letters are meant to be a potluck entry to add a little more flavor to the table.

Solomon said, "There is nothing new under the sun." And indeed, encouraging pastors is not a new idea. Just a necessary one.

Ron Walters

1

Let Them Know That You Were There

———

History calls the Pharos Lighthouse one of the Seven Wonders of the World. It was indeed an engineering marvel, and an early tourist attraction in Egypt. Located on a small peninsula near Alexandria, its forty-five-story, multi-shaped walls were the dominant feature on the local cosmopolitan skyline. The observation deck, complete with a café, was a must-see for all visitors. And, because it was the world's tallest building, the lighthouse served as the crown jewel for the city's tourism and marketing plan. In fact, its famous likeness was even printed on Roman coins.

But the lighthouse was more than just show. It was also practical. It housed a large curved mirror in the beacon chamber and was used to project a one hundred-mile beam of light into the dark Mediterranean night to distressed, searching sailors. The famed structure was built two centuries before Christ and lasted for more than a thousand years beyond. In all of antiquity nothing was as efficient as the Pharos Lighthouse.

And yet, with all the lighthouse's notoriety, its builder might have been forever forgotten had it not been for some quick thinking and gutsy maneuvering. Sostrates was the tower's creator, chief builder, and architect. He gave twenty years of his life to complete the project.

As is true with most builders, Sostrates wished to leave his mark on his life's work. He petitioned Ptolemy II, king of Egypt, for the right to inscribe his name in the marble base of the lighthouse.

But Ptolemy, who was no dummy, would have nothing to do with Sostrates' request. In fact, Ptolemy wanted the lighthouse to bear his own name so that history might remember him, instead of the builder, for the impressive work. Ptolemy demanded that Sostrates chisel the inscription to honor Egypt's king, and no one else. The order was final. The words were scripted and approved. Ptolemy was to be forever remembered, while Sostrates was relegated to be the inscriber of Ptolemy's eternal tribute.

Sostrates was ticked. He had done all the work and yet the king wanted all the credit.

He returned to the job site and devised a plan. Hanging a large curtain to hide his work, he chiseled into the marble these words: BUILT BY SOSTRATES SON OF DEXIPHANES OF KNIDOS ON BEHALF OF ALL MARINERS AND TO THEIR SAVIOR GODS. But then he covered the inscription with some cheap plaster. And in the plaster he wrote the entire text of Ptolemy's self-serving announcement.

As years passed, wind, rain, and pounding surf chipped away the cheap plaster, revealing the name of its true builder.

In a wonderful way, Sostrates' lighthouse is a parable of the church, which belongs to Christ and always will. It will always have His name written upon it. After all, He built it, He bought it, He is the head of it, and He serves as the chief cornerstone. So secure has Christ made His church that "the gates of hell shall not prevail against it."

Here, in the twenty-first century, He has put us in charge of His beloved church. You and I are commissioned to "the building up of the body of Christ."

Take ownership of it. Claim it as your own. Carve your name just below His. Leave your indelible mark for future generations to see. Let it be known that you were there. Be a steward who is worthy of being remembered.

2

God is Not in a Hurry

—⟋⟋⟋—

To an eagle, timing is everything: There's a time to build a nest, a time to hatch an egg, a time to feed the baby eaglet, and a time to teach this young couch-potato bird how to fly!

Flight school in the eagle family is a big deal. The fun begins as the mother eagle wraps her mighty talons around her young freeloader for his first lift-off. Mother will soar two miles high while her horrified baggage gets his first look at the world. When the time is right she retracts her muscular claws and the young eaglet is on his own, free-falling, tumbling, screaming, and facing certain death as the ground quickly approaches.

But, at the perfect moment, the ever-watching mother tucks her wings and makes a beeline for the panicky kid. She zooms past the tumbling feather ball, levels off, spreads her massive wings, and catches her young on her back. This routine is rehearsed over and over until the eaglet learns to fly.

Using this illustration, God reminded Moses, "I've held you up on eagles' wings and brought you to Myself."

What's true about the eagle is true about God: Timing is everything. God's precise moves, though often questioned, are always calculated. But whereas He's "a friend who sticks closer than a brother," one truth remains: God is never in a hurry. His creation serves as evidence; towering redwoods, blue-ice glaciers, our sun's fuel tank—all speak of a Creator who bides His time. God is simply not in a hurry.

It's not as though God can't go faster. After all, it took Him only six days to create an entire universe. But God's dealings with mankind have always been in real time, and in some cases, real *slow* time. For example:

- God's building project for Noah took one hundred years to complete.
- God's promise to give Abraham and Sarah a child took twenty-five years to fulfill.
- God waited four hundred years before He sprang the Children of Israel from Egypt.

No, God will not be rushed. He even uses a different calendar: "One day is as a thousand years, and a thousand years as one day." In other words, He's time*less*.

Meanwhile, we pastors try to set a fire under God's throne, as though He needs prompting. We see issues that can't wait: a long illness, a smoldering church feud, or a wayward child. We want help with pew-sitting dragons, undisciplined disciples, and divisive staff members. We want to know why our church hasn't blossomed the way other churches have. We've got questions, and the answers are slow in coming.

Sound familiar?

From the patriarchs of old, to the pastors of today, God's leaders have always asked the same questions: "When?" and "Why not now?" To paraphrase His answer to Isaiah, "My timing is not your timing, neither are your deadlines my deadlines."

And yet, His unusual timing is the very thing we boast about most:

- Abraham was resigned to kill Isaac when God provided a ram substitute.
- Joseph was on death row, with no hope of parole, when God orchestrated his promotion to prime minister of Egypt.
- Moses sat between Pharaoh's hard-charging army and an impassable Red Sea. Then God did what He does best. He made a way where there *was* no way.

Timing *is* everything. Our timing is best when we wait on Him. And, like the mother eagle, God may let us free-fall, but He's never lost one of His kids yet.

3

Custer Never Had a Chance

—◠◠—

Custer's Last Stand: Three little words that epitomize complete and utter defeat—except for the victors.

On the otherwise peaceful afternoon of June 25, 1876, Lieutenant Colonel George Armstrong Custer, commanding officer of the U.S. Seventh Cavalry, bivouacked in a postcard-like setting of southeast Montana known as Little Big Horn. His orders were to "subdue the Indian uprising." To Custer that was a license to perform genocide on the Sioux nation. The end result, however, was the most lopsided defeat ever suffered by the United States military.

George Custer was a West Point graduate and a seasoned war strategist. His tactics were often criticized, but never his success ratio. This man knew how to wage war—and win.

So, how was this expertly trained and highly decorated veteran out-planned, out-foxed, and out-fought by some of history's most independent and disjointed people?

The answer comes in the name of one man: Chief Sitting Bull, the spiritual leader among the fractured Sioux nation. Though he had neither a formal education nor charismatic sway, he defined his nation's purpose and vision. His leadership was built upon humility. Wisdom and persuasion were his calling cards.

For years he had warned his people of the impending trespass of the white man, of the broken treaties, of the needless killing of ta tanka (the buffalo). He spoke with passion and vivid imagery. Picking up a pinch of earth, he said he would not give up "even this much" of the Black Hills to such a murderous people.

But the Sioux leaders were tired and discouraged. Failed promises had left open wounds and ugly scars. "Nothing will stop the white man's migration," they said. "The Great White Father has too many sons to fight."

But Sitting Bull would not give in. He turned his attention to the new generation of rising Sioux stars. He appealed to their idealism and energy. To *Four Horns*, the philosophical conscience of the younger Sioux, he spoke of social justice. "Can a people who slaughter ta tanka be trusted?" To *Gall*, the strongest warrior, he asked, "Will you allow others to wrestle away your dignity? To *Crazy Horse*, the military phenom, he demanded, "Will you stand by and watch your heritage be destroyed?"

Finally, Sitting Bull issued a call for all Sioux to stand and fight in the sacred land of The Greasy Grass—Little Big Horn—to honor the legacy of their ancestors. To reject his invitation would be to disinherit their past. By battling the Blue Coats on that sacred ground the Sioux could draw strength from former generations. If they died there it would honor their nation's cause. But if they won it would perpetuate their manifest destiny. And so they fought as no army had ever fought.

Custer never had a chance. Sitting Bull's persuasive vision made sure of that.

Every generation has had its visionary leaders like Sitting Bull—those who were forced to prod the naysayers in order to do the unthinkable. Jeremiah was like that; for forty years he faithfully proclaimed God's judgment on apostate Judah, all the while enduring opposition. Isaiah's bio reads the same, as does Hosea's and Amos' and Joel's. And though the response was rarely promising, the prophets' resolve never wavered.

Today we are that tribe of passion-filled leaders—faithful men and women armed with a beacon, turning darkness into light. We may be outnumbered, but neither a hostile culture nor an apathetic church has ever been safe when God's men with vision were unleashed. As the pint-size shepherd said as he took on the giant, "For the battle is the Lord's and He will give you into our hands."

4

Do Not Lose Heart

—⁓—

To the poet, it's the vault in which dreams are kept. To the athlete, it's the high-test fuel that propels the body. To the romantic, it's a gift to be given. To the zealot, it's what's worn on the sleeve. To the physician, it's a muscle extraordinaire. And, to the pastor, it's why the work week never stops at forty hours.

The heart—the unseen, non-negotiable center of human life.

Like an eager kid waving his hand during show-and-tell, the heart beats in the chest, eager to be recognized. And with good reason too. Though it weighs less than a pound, it's the most durable muscle in the body, beating 100,000 times every day. It's only the size of a clenched fist and yet every 20 seconds it receives, cleans, and pumps 6 quarts of blood through every nook and cranny of the body. The energy it exerts is equivalent to lifting 1.5 tons 1 foot off the floor every hour.

Because of the heart's importance, physicians have tried to fix sick hearts for centuries—some with extraordinary results, others not so successful. For example:

- In 350 B.C., the first blood letting office was opened in Alexandria. Egyptian physicians hoped to eliminate heart diseases by eliminating diseased blood.
- In 1785, dried foxglove leaves were mulched into digitalis for the first time. This ingested powder stimulated the heart to create a regular beat.
- In 1903, the electrocardiograph was developed to detect and record the electrical activities of the heart.
- In 1952, the first open-heart surgery was performed.

- In 1982, the artificial heart, Jarvic-7, was implanted. The longest living recipient survived 600 days.
- In 1988, the first Hemopump was used allowing patients to live without a pulse thereby giving the heart time to heal before it started pumping again.
- In 2003, there were 2,300 successful heart transplants in the United States. Another 800 were not as fortunate.

Pastors are also in the heart fixing business. But our work has nothing to do with blocked arteries or damaged myocardium. Our challenge is to operate on the very deadly *hardened* hearts.

Our surgical tools are timeless and effective. "The word of God is living and active, sharper than any two-edged *scalpel*, cutting deep to the soul and the spirit…to the thoughts and attitudes of the heart, exposing us for what we really are."

It's little wonder that almost one thousand verses of Scripture speak of the heart. God's Word has an uncanny ability to cut out sin and weaknesses. It binds wounded spirits and resuscitates weakened hearts. It gives birth to hope. It empowers once-dormant muscles. It revitalizes lost disciplines.

But heart check-ups aren't just for parishioners: Scripture offers an EKG for pastors too. The warnings signs for *pastoral heart disease* can be found in five pressure-point areas:
1.) Don't let the heart be snared by attractive evils.
2.) Don't let the heart be vindictive in another's misfortune.
3.) Don't let the heart be troubled when God's plans supersede our own.
4.) Don't let the heart be bought by the highest bidder.
5.) Don't let the heart wander into complacency.

Heart surgery, whether on a congregation or its pastor, is serious business. Though the needs may be great, the solutions are available. "Do not lose heart."

5

How to Coax Lightning out of a Cloud

—∿—

A violent thunderstorm is not your average kite-flying weather. But neither was Benjamin Franklin your average kite flyer. Yet on one stormy night in 1752 the bespectacled inventor ventured outside with a makeshift kite, a trusty ball of string, and his house key.

Whereas kite flying is typically associated with children and picnics, this was definitely no picnic for ol' Ben. Franklin—who reasoned like Albert Einstein but acted like Evel Knievel—was out to test a highly controversial theory, soon to be called the Philadelphia Experiments. He believed that lightning was simply a discharge of electricity—a lot of electricity. Today we know he was right.

Lightning bolts can measure up to 90 miles long. And, whereas they're only 5 to 6 inches at the core, each bolt literally burns a 15-foot-wide electrified region around its core to about 54,000 degrees Fahrenheit—several times hotter than the surface of the sun. Lightning, and its 1 billion volts of energy, travels at 60,000 miles per second. It's not uncommon for a single bolt to have as many as 40 discharges simultaneously. Lightning is one of nature's most dramatic and dangerous light shows.

Lightning's awesome power is no toy, as Ben found out in a separate experiment. He was curious to know the effects of lightning on a full-grown turkey. So an unsuspecting bird was found and secured to a poorly designed lightning rod. Sure enough, as a lightning bolt struck the rod and sent its supercharged current down the faulty cable, a wayward spark jumped and badly burned the elder statesman. Less fortunate was the turkey. He was immediately incinerated.

Perhaps these experiments were the reason Mr. Franklin established America's first Fire Department, as well as the world's first Fire Insurance Company. No doubt, Ben's half-charred, albeit, well-insured laboratory was a familiar stop for the Philadelphia bucket brigade.

Franklin was ahead of his time, to be sure. Critics formed a long line to take pot-shots at his electro-charged theory. Conventional wisdom had long believed that lightning was simply "an unruly species of atmospheric fire." Few are the men who have dared to challenge society's prevailing opinions. Ben's eccentric views were fuel for ridicule on two continents. "Electricity, indeed!" they scoffed.

As worthy a leader as Ben Franklin was, and as revolutionary as his Philadelphia Experiments became, neither compare to the challenge and thrill of our work. Championing meteorology is heady stuff, to be sure, but declaring God's Word is even more so.

Proclaimers of the truth have the ultimate task: Give people the words they don't want to hear, about a love they do not deserve, from a God they don't want to believe.

It's no wonder the degree of difficulty in preaching is so high. The art of "rightly dividing the word of truth" is a little more complex than flying a kite. Describing an invisible God to a blind world is more involved than coaxing lightning out of a cloud. "Equipping the saints for the work of ministry" requires special gifts. Turkey-torching doesn't.

Today and every day, somewhere on earth, lightning will strike one hundred times, every second. And with the same intensity, today and every day, somewhere on earth, the Spirit of God will strike millions of human hearts in an effort to introduce them to God's love. Each of those whom He touches will need a bright and daring mentor to teach them of the wonder of knowing this God. And that's where we come in.

Don't you love this work?

6

Dirty Hands Won't Do

—m—

Expectant mothers in nineteenth-century Austria must have dreaded a trip to Vienna General Hospital. The death rate at General was five times higher than that of women who chose to have their babies at home. The maternity ward was no place for flowers; they'd all wilt. Instead of a stork on the hospital letterhead, it should have had a buzzard.

But in 1846 all that began to change. That was the year Dr. Ignaz Phillip Semmelweis (Zem-ul-vice) became the assistant obstetrician at Vienna General, the largest hospital and medical school of its kind in the world. Up to that point Vienna General birthed more babies than any hospital in Europe. But almost one in three mothers died in the process.

History has called it "The Childbed Fever." Vienna General called it "bad luck."

Austrian administrators were quick to shift the blame. They determined the high death rate was due to foreign-born doctors who were "rougher in their examinations than the Viennese." So they fired all foreigners. But the death rates didn't change.

Young Dr. Semmelweis had a theory: For months he'd watched scores of doctors go directly from autopsies of cadavers in the morgue to the birthing of babies in obstetrics—without washing their hands. Medical science had not yet learned the dangers of an unwashed examiner's hand.

But the crusade for cleaner hands fell on deaf ears.

The official hospital response was, "It is sheer impertinence to suggest that the finest doctors in the world should carry contagion upon their hands." And, with that, they fired Semmelweis.

Sometimes, identifying dirty hands can be costly.

But Semmelweis continued the cause. In a debate he said, "I have shown you how the mothers are infected. I have also shown how it can be prevented. I have proven all that I've said. But while we talk, talk, talk, women are dying. I am not asking for anything earthshaking. I'm just asking you to wash. For God's sake, wash your hands!"

Unwashed hands are deadly tools. And not just in hospitals. The same is true in the church. Our mission to "preach the Word" is to identify unwashed hands and point to the soap. We're to "admonish every man and teach every man with all wisdom, that we may present every man [washed and clean] in Christ."

It's always been that way:

- For a year David had dodged the scandal about Bathsheba and her late husband. Then up stepped the prophet Nathan, who said, "Thou art the man!"
- Saul lied about his unsuccessful mission to destroy Agag and the Amalekites. Then up stepped Samuel to ask, "Why didn't you obey God's orders?"
- Israel seemed content to worship God through sterile traditions and ceremony. Then up stepped John the Baptist, who challenged them to cleanse their hearts.
- When the legalistic Jews intimidated Peter, he shunned the Gentile believers and discredited the doctrine of salvation by God's grace alone, even though he knew better. Then up stepped Paul, who "withstood him to his face."

Identifying the dirt and pointing to the eternal soap is what we do. The tried-and-true forgiveness of God, made possible through Christ, is His best offer yet. It's a grace that doesn't dissolve. And the story—which is ours to tell—of His willing ability to remove deep, stubborn stains never grows old. It's a story with the perfect ending: He "creates in us a clean heart" and makes us "whiter than snow."

7

The Body Extraordinaire

—∽∿∽—

The human body is the one piece of creation most like the Creator. We're made in His image, an ineffably high and lofty position. Therefore, you'd expect our anatomy to showcase extraordinary efficiencies as well as profound spiritual implications. And it does. Consider this:

- A baby is born with 350 bones, but by the time he's my age he'll have, and need, only 206. Additionally, a growing child replaces his bone mass at the rate of 100% every year; in adulthood that rate is only 18%.
- The average person is wrapped in nine pounds of skin that is reproducing. It is forever shedding the old, outer layer, revealing the ever-changing *new you*. In a lifetime we will own about 1,000 different skin covers.
- The stomach produces a powerful acid that's strong enough to dissolve zinc. As a result, this digestive agent destroys a half-million cells on the stomach lining every minute. Yet the stomach quietly replaces them at the same rate. In fact, the entire stomach lining is replaced every three days.
- An adult's head is 15% of the body mass, uses 20% of the body's oxygen and 15% of the body's blood, yet, amazingly, accounts for only 2% of the body's weight.

But the human body is more than a series of independent systems, each concerned with its own well being. There's a common bond within the body, an order to its greatness.

Organizationally, the body does what the brain wants. The brain serves as control-central for zillions of cells working in a myriad ways to multitask the body's multitude of priorities. Case in point:

- Slide into a hot bath and immediately your body's nerve-center will collect data from every location and report the condition of each comfort zone to your brain. As the water temperature increases, the brain continues to gather and analyze the incoming nerve impulses. When the water reaches exactly 115 degrees, the brain will immediately dispatch an urgent message to every muscle in your body: "Get out! Get out! Get out!"

The psalmist wasn't kidding when he said, "I am fearfully and wonderfully made."

But our body wasn't meant to serve only as a carton for human life. It was also designed to be a brilliant metaphor of God and His people. "He appointed Christ to be head over everything regarding the church, which is His body."

The body of Christ—the church—is to be the physical expression of the head—Christ. He sends the messages, and His people respond.

There are times, however, when outside influences override the brain; when foreign stimulants hot-wire the body's system, causing an independent reaction. For example, if a doctor's rubber mallet hits your knee in the right place, your leg will kick. Even if your brain tells it not to, it will.

Sometimes the church is like that. Christ's body has always been the target of vicious hammers looking for nerves that will cause the body to react independently of the head. The Galatians were like that: They were hit with false teaching and reacted badly. Likewise, the Corinthians were struck with worldliness and reacted badly. Even some Philippians were hit with the mallet of disunity and reacted badly. But, in each case, a teacher of God's Word guided them through the pain and negative reflexes.

Today it's our turn. We're the teachers called upon to keep the body focused on what's important to the Head. We're to "proclaim Him, admonishing and teaching everyone with all wisdom, so that we may present everyone perfect in Christ."

8

Before I Go...

—⁓—

Famous last words: those deathbed monologues that refuse to succumb; verbal *coups de grace* that ensure immortality. With apologies to Art Linkletter, kids don't say the darnedest things, dying people do. The final farewells of us mortals speak volumes about our life's work and eternal preparedness.

Some sojourners actually look forward to death. For example, David Livingstone, the Scottish missionary to Africa, died saying, "Build me a hut, for at last I am going home." Others, however, are less secure as they breathe their last. Napoleon, for one, seemed disoriented by his final enemy. "France...Army...General...Josephine," was all he could say before he died. Edgar Allan Poe, who was never at a loss for words, was tongue tied. His last breath was, "Rest, shore, no more." (At least it rhymed.)

Ironically, some last words appear almost rehearsed, as did Charles Darwin's: "I am not the least bit afraid to die." But others are more spontaneous, such as D.L. Moody's: "I see earth receding. Heaven is opening. God is calling me."

Of course there are those who treat death nonchalantly. Marie Antoinette, after intentionally stomping on her executioner's foot, said with sarcasm, "Oh, I beg your pardon, sir. Please, please forgive me." Socrates' last words were to a disciple: "We owe a chicken to Ascleposis. Pay it and don't forget." The famed Greek mathematician, Archimedes, was busy solving a geometric riddle when ordered to follow the Roman death squad. "Wait," he demanded, "till I am finished with this puzzle."

Others hope to delay the grim reaper's visit. Queen Elizabeth ruled half the world in 1603 yet died saying, "All my possessions I will give for more time." Likewise, Voltaire, the renowned French infidel, told his physician, "I will give you half of what I'm worth if you will give me six more months of life. But even then, I'm convinced I will go to hell."

Some play the cynic while dying. Beethoven joked, "Clap now, my friends, the comedy is done." Sir Walter Raleigh, though less flippant, was nevertheless ghoulish with his executioner. "Your ax gives me no fear. It is simply a sharp medicine to cure all my diseases."

And then there are those who see death as the beginning of a blessed hope. "Lord, shall I die? Shall I die?" asked Augustine, before answering his own question, "Yes, Lord, why not now?" Martin Luther breathed his last while quoting Psalm 68, "God is the Lord by whom we escape death." George Whitefield, the great evangelist of the 1700s, passed into eternity saying, "Lord Jesus, I am weary *in* thy work, but not *of* thy work." And William Carey, the father of modern missions, programmed his own funeral, saying, "When I am gone, speak nothing of Dr. Carey. Speak only of Dr. Carey's Savior."

A person's last words tend to unmask that person's true identity. That's why our job is so critical. Many people will enter eternity with the truth we've taught them on their lips. Our teaching has long-term effects, the ultimate staying power. Paul described it as, "Admonishing every man and teaching every man…that we may present every man perfect in Christ." Simply put, our mission is to prepare men and women for a face-to-face appointment with God.

And, faithfully fulfilling that assignment, we will hear another set of famous last words, "Well done, thou good and faithful servant."

What a day that will be!

9

Through the Eyes of a Visionary

—∭—

- visionary (vizh'ə-nĕr'ē) adj. 1. Given to, or characterized by, fanciful or impractical ideas. 2. A dreamer. 3. Not practical.

Now there's a definition that slipped past the proofreader. If visionaries are *impractical dreamers*, then the publishers of the new Webster's Dictionary named their book for the wrong guy.

Noah Webster personified a visionary. He spent 20 years fulfilling his *impractical idea* by creating a dictionary with American pronunciations and usages, as distinguished from its British counterpart. His historic work introduced 12,000 words never before listed in any dictionary. Presumably, *visionary* was included, but with a different definition.

Today's editors have confused "visionaries" with "wishful thinkers." Visionaries aren't impractical people; they're just more experienced travelers to the land of *What if…?* Whereas most people use their eyes for looking, visionaries use theirs to see.

In 1970, a wide-eyed thirty-year-old, Michael Viner, was desperate to make a splash in the competitive music recording industry. Without resources and contacts, he spent his life's savings to press several thousand copies of an album titled *The Best of Marcel Marceau*. It was a thirty-five-minute platter of silence interrupted by occasional applause. But rather than promote it through the usual route of the broadcasting and recording industries, Viner sent his prank records to publishers. *Newsweek* and *Billboard* magazines ran the story, as did every major newspaper, touting Viner's bizarre project.

Mail orders for *The Best of Marcel Marceau* began pouring in. And in the end Viner's newfound capital allowed him to produce the serious music he'd always dreamed of. Michael Viner was a visionary.

But the truest list of visionaries is found in God's leadership roll call: faithful followers with impractical ideas who saw things different than most.

- Twelve spies scouted out the Promised Land and brought their reports to Moses. Ten of the spies saw giants and, with typical vision-killing instincts, concluded victory was impossible. Caleb and Joshua, however, reported the same giants but said, "Because they're so big they'll be easier to hit. We'll bring them down!" Visionaries talk like that.

- In a classic attempt at overkill, the massive Syrian army circled Elisha's bungalow for revenge. The prophet, through what appeared to be divine wiretap, had thwarted every Syrian battle plan. Elisha's servant became unglued when he spotted the enemy so near. "What's the problem?" Elisha wondered. "These men are no match for our unseen army of angels." Visionaries have resources undetected by the world.

- For fifteen years the Jerusalem Construction Company had blankly stared at their city in ruins. To rebuild seemed hopeless. Then Nehemiah showed up, assessed the situation, organized the crews, and the city began to rise. Visionaries are focused.

- Noah was no different. For one hundred years he clocked in at the shipyard. It didn't matter that it had never rained, or that he lived hundreds of miles from the nearest body of water, or that no one else had the same passion for boating. Visionaries are typically a minority, undeterred by the criticism of others.

Pastors are called to be visionaries too. We're His signposts, the visible agents for an invisible God. We teach people to follow a God whose audible voice they've never heard, to love a Savior whose face they've never seen, to live according to a Book whose authenticity is forever attacked, and to plan an eternity in a place they've never been.

Only a wide-eyed visionary can do that.

10

Finding Leadership Through a Sea of Hands

—⟋⟍—

The whole world was embroiled in a war whose outcome was very much in doubt. Nazi Germany had braced itself for a long and deadly battle. But before the good guys would counter with a plan to crush Hitler's European campaign, a leader would have to be picked.

Throughout time only a few candidates will ever be offered such historic roles. In 1943, leading the allied conquest would become the world's most important assignment.

President Roosevelt had a handful of talented military strategists to choose from: MacArthur and Patton were the American frontrunners, and Field Marshall Montgomery was the British favorite. Each had earned enough medals to armor-plate a small tank, and each was lobbying for the job. But the more they jockeyed, the more suspicious the president became. They were interested in reputations and headlines; Roosevelt was interested in winning a war.

Leadership isn't a birthright; nor is it always given to the most impressive. Just ask David's oldest brother, Eliab. He fit the profile perfectly but he couldn't hold a candle to his skinny-armed, melancholic sibling.

More often than not, history's best leaders were the ones who never desired the job.

Roosevelt's surprise choice was a younger, quieter, dark-horse candidate, the highly detailed general from Kansas, Dwight David Eisenhower. And the critics howled. He just didn't fit the profile. To make matters worse, most of his wartime expertise was from an air conditioned office in Washington, D.C. During the first year of WWII he was shuffling papers at the Pentagon.

But Eisenhower was the right man for the job.

The truest leaders will often rise to the top via a road less traveled. Notre Dame University, for example, has repeatedly warned its "A" students to get to know the "D" students. The school's research has shown that their honor students may very likely be employed someday by their dropouts.

Biblical leadership operates along the same line. God rarely recruits from the most-likely-to-succeed crowd. Instead, He uses "the foolish things of this world to confuse the wise." The list of examples is endless.

Conversely, when He did go with a BMOC, chaos invariably followed. Leaders such as Samson and King Saul were quick starters but neither was a closer. On paper they looked good. Each was Magna Cum Loaded. Yet in the final analysis, when tested, leadership ate them alive.

On the occasions when elite candidates did survive, it had much to do with their education at Humble State. It's a prerequisite for all who serve. Paul, for example, pulled duty in the Sahara Desert for three years. Moses was dispatched to the world's most remote outpost for forty years. It was only in solitude that God could reshape them into the leaders they would become.

But typically God chooses the least-likelies to accomplish His work; the common laborer to do His kingdom building. He picked Gideon, though he displayed serious signs of cowardice. He picked Nehemiah, who was employed as an expendable food taster. He picked Jonah, though he had no heart for the job. He picked Peter, though he was forever talking first and thinking later. Each recruit broke the mold, a second stringer at best. At first glance they were throwaways. Yet each one accomplished great things.

Biblical leadership is unlike any other assignment. The obstacles are bigger. The stakes are higher. The cost is greater. And whereas most have never heard His call, we have.

Aren't you glad He picked you?

11

What do Birds and Leaders have in Common?

—⁓—

In the years following the American Revolution, our nation's decision makers solicited new ideas for the purpose of national imaging. The colonists had just bumped off the world's most powerful military machine. The little-country-that-could was in need of a new face, a look that would say, "Move over world, there's a new kid on the block."

Nominations were made and votes were cast for monikers that would define who we are. A flag had already been chosen, but we still needed an anthem, an emblem, a motto. For the most part, choices were obvious and selections were easy.

However, the debate stalled on one seemingly insignificant item— the national bird. The issue may have been low on the agenda, but it was high with emotion. The odds-on favorite was the bald eagle, so strong, so impressive, so American, so…

But one impassioned and dissenting voice came from America's elder statesman, Benjamin Franklin. The old printer had nothing against the proud eagle, but he believed another feathered friend was more deserving—the all-American turkey.

That's when fireworks began. The bird debate grew hot and heavy. It was the barnyard challenging Wild Kingdom. It created a fiery exchange with politicians arguing beak to beak.

Ol' Ben was quite adamant about his nominee, albeit unsuccessful. The turkey lost by a landslide. But Ben may have been onto something with all his turkey talk. Consider this:

- Turkeys can grow to 86 mouthwatering pounds and top out at 3,500 feathers. The average eagle tips the Toledos at only 15 pounds but carries 7,000 feathers. In other words the turkey is more substance, the eagle more fluff.
- The turkey was the featured guest at the first dinner on the moon with astronauts Neil Armstrong and Buzz Aldrin.
- Turkeys have a rhythmic gobble. Eagles scream a high-pitched, car alarm shrill.
- Turkeys can run up to 25 miles per hour. Eagles don't even try.
- Each American consumes 19 lbs. of turkey annually. It's a felony to eat an eagle.

Here's more support for the underdog bird: The dictionary defines a turkey as "A large bird raised for food." In other words, he exists **for** others. The same dictionary says the eagle is "a large bird of prey." He exists **because** of others. Or, better put, the turkey came to minister, while the eagle came to be ministered unto.

Okay, okay, so I'm stretching the point! But there is a principle here.

Picking our leaders—like our symbols—is often done by appearance. Young David was a classic example. He was completely overlooked as Israel's king-elect because the prophet Samuel—a man who should have known better—was more enamored of David's aristocratic-looking brother. But the Lord was not impressed. All that glitters is not God's.

Jesus picked His twelve disciples not because of who they were but because of what they would become. The issue wasn't *their worth* but rather *His work*.

In fact, the Twelve thought of themselves as eagles, though Jesus never did. They wanted to talk about greatness but He wanted them to learn humility. They wanted to rule but He wanted to wash feet. They lobbied for position but He taught them to serve. And, in time, they followed His lead. There would be no prima donnas on His team.

The curriculum He used then He still uses today. His charge to leaders has always been, and will always be, "Follow Me."

12

Next Year in Jerusalem!

—ᴍ—

For nearly two thousand years, Jews in every corner of the globe have ended their Passover Seder with the ritual line, "Next year in Jerusalem." That rallying call expressed the ancient hope of all Jews—a passion to return one day to their ancestral home; a burning wish that nineteen centuries of persecution had failed to extinguish.

They waited and waited. And the wait was worth it.

On May 14, 1948, at 4 o'clock in the afternoon, a black sedan pulled up to the Tel Aviv Museum on Rothschild Boulevard. Out stepped David Ben-Gurion, the bantam-sized Jewish warrior and soon-to-be prime minister. He bounded up the marble steps, saluted the military guards, and took his place at the podium under two enormous Star-of-David flags in the main hall of the museum.

Ben-Gurion (meaning "son of the lion cub") slowly panned the crowd of dignitaries and journalists, sensing the historic occasion of the moment. In a deliberate, sometimes broken voice he began to read aloud Israel's Declaration of Independence to a visibly moved audience. In part it read:

> On November 29, 1947, the General Assembly of the United Nations adopted a resolution providing for an independent Jewish state in Palestine…As a result, we, the members of the National Council, representing the Jewish people in Palestine and the world Zionist movement, are united today at a solemn assembly.
>
> In the light of natural law and the history of the Jewish people, as well as in accordance with the resolution of the United Nations,

we proclaim the foundation of the Jewish state in the Holy Land
which will bear henceforth the name of "The State of Israel."
It will be founded on the principles of liberty, justice and peace,
just as they were conceived by the prophets of Israel...."

When Ben-Gurion concluded the reading, the thirty-seven members of the National Council signed the document, many as they wept uncontrollably.

Israel had waited and waited, but now the wait was over. The country was theirs again.

Millenniums before, another wait was on. The prophets had endured a similar longing, but for a different reason. God had made them special agents to distribute news-breaks for the coming Messiah. As they wrote the words, they ached to see the day when "a virgin will conceive and a bear a son, and...call His name Immanuel (God with us)." They yearned to be on location when the Savior arrived: "Bethlehem...out of you shall He come forth." They told of His forerunner, His mission, His ministry, His teaching, His triumphal entry, His rejection, His betrayal, His death, His resurrection, His ascension, and three hundred other specifics. And...they waited.

And, at the perfect time, the eventful announcement came: "I bring you good news of a great joy that will be for all people. For today in the city of David there has been born for you a Savior, who is Christ the Lord. And this will be a sign for you: you will find a baby wrapped in cloths, and lying in a manger."

The wait for the Messiah was finally over. In a small but predetermined town, in a humble stable, in one ordinary trough was placed the hope of the world, and His name was called "Wonderful Counselor, Mighty God, Everlasting Father, Prince of Peace."

That announcement, first proclaimed by angels, is now ours to share. There can be no better news and no greater joy: the Savior of the world has been born. God is indeed with us.

The wait was worth it.

13

The Fine Art of Bible Spelunking

—⟨⟨⟨—

An old friend called the other day, ordering me to pull on my rattiest Levi's and dirtiest boots because he was taking me spelunking. "Spe-whating?" I asked. My mind drew a complete blank. I thumbed my Webster's to the S's to find s-p...s-p-e-l...s-p-e-l-u-n-k-i-n-g (pronounced **spee-_lung_-king**) and read: "the exploring of caves."

Spelunking is a bonafide sport, practiced around the world by an unusual breed of sub-surface hikers. Those in the know call them "cavers" or "potholers." The more I read, the more intrigued I became.

A spelunker is happier in a thousand-foot shaft than in a swanky restaurant. He breathes deep to fill his lungs with rich, damp, musty air. What we call claustrophobia, he calls cozy. His favorite bird is a bat. Wiggling through an underground crevasse is pure ecstasy.

Spelunking tools for this subterranean insanity include a lighted hardhat, boots, pads, and ropes. This sportsman has every appearance of an underground, bungee-jumping coalminer.

As I looked closer, I noticed that a spelunker resembled a pastor-teacher.

It's not difficult to see the similarity between those who explore underground passageways and those who live in church corridors. Neither counts the hours, but, for safety's sake, both keep a constant eye on their trusty compass. Each has an insatiable appetite to go deeper than ever before. And both wonder why more surface dwellers don't take the journey with them.

That's because both the spelunker and the pastor have tasted the thrill of going where few have gone. One searches darkened caves for nature's clues. The other searches God's Word ("…a lamp to [our] feet and a light for [our] path") to solve problems with eternal answers. And both discover hidden treasures found nowhere else.

A spelunker talks in code. For example, if he announces that he's found a kitchen sink, a bathtub, and a showerhead, an inexperienced civilian might assume he's been to Home Depot. If he says he's looking for bacon, popcorn, and pudding, few would know he's searching for rare and natural mineral formations found deep inside the earth's crust.

In the same manner, pastors live with code-like phrases: "He must increase and I must decrease" is our constant prayer. "Study to show yourself approved" is our daily assignment. "Preach the word, be ready in season and out of season" is our permanent job description. "I have fought the good fight, I have finished the course" is our goal. "Well done thou good and faithful servant" is our finish line.

Seminary is where most of us pastors were taught to explore. Our Bible spelunking came as we learned from veterans who opened The Book and taught us about our awesome God. And today *we're* the veterans to the next generation of explorers. Each week our studies take us deep into God's Word to find truth, and each weekend we resurface to unveil for others God's many-colored mysteries. Then, on Monday, we re-enter the cavernous depths of Scripture to uncover more.

What an adventuresome work we have. Just like spelunkers, we have our ups and downs. At times we come home bruised and exhausted, with little to show for our efforts. Routinely, we get tired *in* this work, yet never *of* it. But our constant searches through God's Word, and the privilege to discover its beauty, are rewards in themselves.

Who could ask for a more exciting assignment?

14

Yours To Count On

—◆—

Jeb Stuart was the Civil War's version of a B-2 Stealth Bomber. This gutsy West Point grad had the uncanny ability to infiltrate enemy lines without being detected. He was nicknamed "the eyes of the army" and was unquestionably General Robert E. Lee's most trusted soldier.

During the June 1862 defense of Richmond, General Lee sent Stuart to scout and assess the right flank of General McClelland's Federal Army. Stuart not only achieved his mission but rode completely around McClelland's troops to deliver a comprehensive report to Lee.

In his next campaign Stuart was ordered to infiltrate enemy lines and to destroy a large cache of Union weapons and supplies. But, while there, Stuart confiscated secret documents showing the strength and position of other Federal forces.

Stuart's bravery and extraordinary skill as an intelligence officer were unparalleled in Civil War battles. And with each mission Stuart would submit his report to Lee, signed "Yours to count on, Jeb Stuart."

In every battle and in every war there are those who can be counted on. Many wear the uniform but only a handful stand out as heroes—those who go beyond the call of duty. And those are a rare breed indeed.

The church produces the same kind of heroes from its battlefields. They too are the ones who accept the road less traveled. They're uncommon men and women "of whom the world was [and is] not worthy." They're champions who can be counted on.

- In the third century, church theologian Origen was the target of vicious attacks by the vile Greek emperor Decius, who hoped to discredit Origen's character and teaching with accusations of immorality. To further safeguard his testimony, Origen castrated himself in order to protect the gospel from any possible scandal.

- In the fourth century, Ambrose led the church in its fight for survival against hostile heretics. In a daring move he challenged the Catholic emperor Theodosius to do public penance for his slaughter of seven thousand lives at the Thessalonican circus, insisting that the emperor may be "*within* the church, but not *over* the church." His bold move powerfully impressed a local pagan leader, a young man named Augustine. All because Ambrose could be counted on.

- In the fifth century, John Chrysostom, the leading biblical expositor of his day, was kidnapped and carted off to Constantinople because the Roman hierarchy determined he should be their archbishop. Rather than protest his forced promotion Chrysostom preached a painfully direct message to the city's royalty. Soon he was banished by the emperor's wife, Eudosia, for insulting her. He had the gall to call her a sinner.

Every century has those whom the Savior can count on. Francis of Assisi walked away from wealth in order to kiss the hands of lepers. John Knox endured the ridicule of Mary Queen of Scots in his effort to save Scotland. Dietrich Bonhoeffer turned his silent pulpit into a megaphone in Nazi Germany before suffering Hitler's wrath.

It's a frightening world we minister to. The scoreboard rarely shows us in the lead. There's a great temptation to take the easy way out, to slow down, or water down, or calm down.

But our assignment has never changed: "To fight the good fight, to finish the course, to keep the faith." To be able to say to our Master, "Yours to count on, Lord!"

15

A Deafening Hum

—m—

Six years ago scientific instruments discovered a mysterious and irritating hum reverberating throughout the earth. Though its pitch was too low for humans to hear, monitoring technology heard the bedrock bedlam loud and clear. On a musical scale the seismic note comes in at sixteen octaves below middle C.

Actually, we're fortunate to be unable to hear it. The boorish tones vary from corner to earth's corner, and when blended together they harmonize like a chorus of angry whales with a bad case of laryngitis.

At first sound there was a mad scientific dash to identify the electronic brawl. And now the mystery has been solved. With earplugs in hand, science has uncovered these underground belches.

The *hum*, they say, is birthed in a simple ocean wave. Each wave's swirling motion, when joined with other waves, creates a rolling barrel effect. When these lazy watery rolls meet with foul weather they're suddenly pressed deep into the sea's belly, pounding like a drum on the ocean's floor, raising the ground by a fraction of an inch as the waves wash by, creating global vibrations which produce the hum.

From a simple wave, to an unheard hum, we learn of the earth's mighty power.

Besides being a scientific discovery, it's a parable about preaching.

Ours is a simple mandate: "To preach the word…in season and out of season." In other words, our Christ-centered message, combined with His forces, will accomplish His work.

It's all about Him. It's never about us.

Take Paul, for instance. He had a bio-sheet to command an audience anywhere at any time. Then, top that off with his great natural abilities. Yet Paul refused to rely on either. "I was with you in weakness and in fear. My speech and my preaching were not with persuasive words of human wisdom, but with a demonstration of the Spirit's power."

The more our message is focused on Him the more it *reverberates*.

Jonathan Edwards was without peer among eighteenth-century preachers. But many have wondered why he chose to read his sermons rather than "deliver" them. The best guess is that he never wanted to be accused of using his persuasive techniques to gain a response. He wanted the message to bring the results, not the messenger.

Even Moses was a believer in this simple recipe. Every time he addressed Pharaoh, Moses began with the words, "Thus says the Lord...." He left no doubt as to who was whom. And the *hum* was deafening.

It was the same with Jeremiah. Though dramatic at times, his simple yet direct message never confused a generation who loved worldliness more than godliness. It was the same with Elijah. Although he continually made the headlines, his prayer remained, "That these people will know that You, oh Lord, are God." It was the same with John, who was determined that "He must increase but I must decrease." *Hummmmm.*

And it was the same with Jesus. Though His generation lived under a bent religious system, with the Pharisees exegeteing the daylights out of the Law, Jesus was simply offering Good News. The distinction was dramatic. The Pharisees spoke of tradition. Jesus spoke of His Father. No wonder the Pharisees feared losing their audience. Jesus was fresh. And the *hum* never stopped.

Some things are felt around the world. A Christ-centered message is one of them.

16

The Limitations of Christ

—✖—

To the casual observer it might appear that Jesus was nomadic, wandering dusty roads from village to village dispensing His humanitarian miracles and pithy sayings—a first-century philanthropist who scattered goodness and golden rules like confetti.

But nothing could be further from the truth. Jesus was the world's most strategic planner. In fact, His organizational skills put an endless universe into constant motion. He designed and molded every living cell. And He alone crafted the world's most enduring institutions, the home and the church being exhibits A and B.

The honored robes of leadership fit perfectly on this humble carpenter from Nazareth.

But it wasn't easy. He was continually bucking the status quo, fighting city hall. From the smear campaigns of the Pharisees to the out-of-sync ideas of His disciples, from the condescension of His family and friends to Satan's most vicious attacks, Jesus was resolute. He knew what He had to do and how He had to do it.

Though He was the omnipotent God, His powerful leadership was, ironically, marked by His limitations. In fact, they became His trademark and continue to serve as the template for every Christian leader since. Mystical they're not. He never intended them to be. But nobody has ever defined successful ministry better.

First, Jesus limited His time to doing only His Father's will. "I have accomplished the work You gave me to do." And He did it unwaveringly, completely, sincerely, willingly, fervently, readily, swiftly, and constantly. He had not come from heaven to recite a well-rehearsed script but to live a life of righteous rebellion. Not only did He preach against sin, He also acted against sin. When His Father's house was profaned He flew into action. God's justice never looked so resolute.

Jesus limited His conversations. Every recorded dialogue was deliberate. No words were wasted; they were customized for each person and every audience. "The words which You gave to Me, I have given to them." And His words struck a cord. To the hurting, He spoke of hope. At a funeral, He spoke of life. To the blind, He spoke of light. To the leper, He offered His touch. And the people loved Him for it.

He limited Himself to a target audience. "I have not come to call the righteous but sinners to repentance." He looked beyond the curiosity seekers and gravitated to the needy. His ministry was one of depth, not breadth. He sequestered His students for in-depth training. He commanded others to "tell no one." He was unshaken when thousands walked away from His teaching. And even when He had an audience with the political power brokers of His day, "He opened not His mouth."

Finally, Jesus was careful to train His replacements. "As you have sent me into the world, I have also sent them into the world." For three years His protégés heard it all, saw it all, and even got on-the-job, hands-on experience in dozens of miraculous works. Jesus held nothing back from them. He schooled them in every phase of ministry. They saw Him laugh, weep, teach, pray, challenge, rest, serve, heal, answer, and lead. And when it was their turn to take leadership, they never asked, "How?" They had already learned that secret from the Master.

The model that served so well for the disciples is the same model for us today. Limit yourself to His priorities and you can't go wrong.

17

Make Believe and Biblical Truth

—⁓—

Physics: The scientific study of *matter* and *energy* and the relationship between the two.

Physicist: The scientist who answers complex physics questions, such as: Why is church attendance never as high as those days when you print a short supply of bulletins?

We owe much to the world's great physicists: Archimedes, whose studies of hydraulics and hydrostatics changed science forever; Sir Isaac Newton, who uncovered the Law of Gravity; and Albert Einstein, whose Theory of Relativity explains how…well…you know.

But the most imaginative of all physicists have to be the Warner Brothers. Their cartoon characters have rewritten every physical law known to man. None of the well-tested laws of physics is sacred to these innovative neo-scientists. Deep within their creative laboratories, with sketchpad and drawing pencil in hand, they've taught us how:

- A body suspended in mid-air will remain in mid-air until the subject is made aware of his plight. At this point the law of gravity will kick in.
- The law of gravity is selective. Everything falls faster than an anvil.
- A body, if moving fast enough, can pass through solid matter, leaving a perfect cookie-cutter hole in said matter.
- During rapid motion, some objects will momentarily appear in a stationary position while the balance of the body continues to

move. This is particularly true during ferocious fights in which a participant's head will suddenly appear while the dizzying skirmish continues.

- During high-speed chases, certain bodies (most often a road runner's) can pass through solid mountains which have been previously painted to resemble a tunnel. Other bodies (most notably a coyote's) cannot.

- Cats possess a cosmic glue that allows them to quickly recover when they've been disassembled, accordion-pleated, dynamited, scared furless, or after they've assumed the shape of any small container they've fallen into.

Rewriting physical laws in cartoons is fun and harmless. But only a Looney-Tune would deny the real thing.

The same thing is true when it comes to Scripture. Changing or ignoring God's Word is a dangerous proposition. And yet many have tried. History is littered with attempted rewrites of biblical truth—or doing away with it altogether, hoping to outsmart the Creator.

Take the third-century Roman emperor Diocletian, for example. He slaughtered so many Christians and burned so many Bibles that he gloated, "The name *Christian* is forever extinguished." Yet five years later his successor, Constantine, declared Christianity as Rome's national religion.

Or Voltaire, the articulate French atheist who promised, "Fifty years from now the world will hear no more of the Bible." But instead, on the fiftieth anniversary of Voltaire's death, the Geneva Bible Society was using Voltaire's house as a print shop to produce more Bibles.

Or Carl Sagan, the noted astronomer, whose bold first sentence of his bestseller, *Cosmos*, states, "The Cosmos is all that is or ever was or ever will be." Sagan died in 1997. If he could rewrite his book today, I'm convinced Dr. Sagan would tell about a whole new dimension of the cosmos that he never considered before.

There will always be dissenters to the truth. Skeptics will continue to critique our message as antiquated, naïve, out of touch, and irrelevant. But they're simply playing the role of cartoonist. Make-believe is still just make-believe. And the Truth will always be the truth.

No matter how loud or clever our culture may be, two things remain true: 1) Road runners cannot pass through solid mountains, and 2) God's Word is always reliable.

18

I Shaved My Back For Nothin' Cuz Nothin's Comin' Back To Me

—◁ɯ▷—

Country & western music: as true an American art form as there ever was. It's the unmistakable beauty of nasal twang on sheet music. It's heart surgery performed on a steel guitar; syllables sliding an entire scale on purpose. It's Nashville's contribution to the Louvre.

Most CW songs tell sad stories. The ballads range from broken hearts to trailer parks, from poker hands to one night stands, with a whole lot of dusty miles in between. But though the venues may vary, the storylines remain the same.

The most popular theme is "My baby done me wrong." This includes such hits as *I'm digging a hole to bury my heart* and *Hog tied over you*. And who could ever forget *Flushed from the bathroom of your heart*, or *I shaved my back for nothin' cuz nothin's comin' back to me*. And, of course, the ever popular *Jesus may love you but I don't, God may forgive you but I won't*.

Another familiar storyline is the "Fallen arches and broken dreams" category. These songs typically translate Murphy's Law into hillbillyese. Old standards like *I'm darned if I don't and danged if I do* and *All my ex's live in Texas*. Colorful classics like *You dirty old egg-suckin dog*, or *Earache my eye*. And the boot-tapping hit *The homecoming queen's got a gun*. And, my personal favorite, *You're the reason my kids are ugly*.

In the world of music, country & western is the lovable-but-ugly sister in the family portrait. It's a chunk of concrete in an upscale china shop. It's TV dinners at Buckingham Palace. Hog-calling at Carnegie Hall. The music's unpretentiousness exposes the soul of its singer. That's the appeal. The musician's heartache transcends our own. His pain is our pain. His dog died too.

I bring this up because of Psalm 7. It's easy to see that David was a big fan of Israel's impassioned music. Psalm 7's introduction identifies it as "A Shiggaion of David." The footnote in my Bible says, "Wild passionate song"—perhaps the Hebrew equivalent to our country & western.

David's mood-filled psalm sets a mournful backdrop. His visual lyrics tell of bad times and bad people with bad motives. His heart is hurting. But even though the psalm begins on a sad note, David's confidence in God refuses to fold. Like a strong musical beat, his faith won't die. Things will get better. True love for the true God will be rewarded in the end.

The music of the Bible, as with country & western, was inescapably locked with life, and with God. Music in Israel was more than a tune to whistle while watching the flock. Much more. It was a weapon in war, a protocol at coronations, and an entrée at feasts. It was a sedative to calm the nerves of overworked prophets. And, as with the psalmist, it was a heavenly frequency that tuned out the world and focused on the Father. Music eased his pain. It was David's Epsom salts. And, as in Psalm 7, it represented his plea for help.

David sang, "O Lord my God, in thee I have taken refuge. Save me from all those who pursue me, and deliver me... If I have done wrong, if there is injustice in my hands, if I have rewarded evil to my friend, then let the enemy pursue my soul and overtake it... Arise, O Lord, lift up Thyself against the rage of my adversaries...Vindicate me, O Lord... I will give thanks to the Lord and will sing praise to the name of the Most High."

Sing it, David. We feel it too!

19

The World's Heavyweight Championship of Leadership

—m—

Leadership comes in all shapes and sizes. Like many things, it's difficult to define but easy to see. Great leadership is rarely measured
by parades or speeches, but by the ability to handle difficult situations
in the worst of times. The bigger the challenge, the better the chance
to evaluate the leader.

The American Revolution, celebrated this month for the 229th time,
was just such an occasion to contrast two very different leaders. It was,
so to speak, the World's Heavyweight Championship of Leadership. I
can hear the ring-announcer now:

> "In the far corner, wearing the impressive purple robes of
> monarchy, the sovereign ruler of Great Britain and the reigning
> World Champion, King George III. And his opponent, in the
> near corner, wearing a triangular hat and short pants, fighting
> for free men everywhere, the challenger from America, citizen
> John Adams."

King George III was not your prototypical leader. Being Britain's
third king in a row named George, he probably just wanted to be
noticed. He decided to play hardball with his long-distance subjects, to
arm-wrestle the indomitable American spirit. This Buckingham bully
chose to ignore England's diplomatic problems by creating new ones.
He was like the auto mechanic who couldn't fix my brakes so he made
my horn louder.

John Adams' leadership style was very much the opposite. This brilliant thinker knew that greatness could not be mandated but was achieved through vision-casting and proper recruiting. Adams' strategy was to paint a three-dimensional picture of freedom and then find the players to bring it to life. And he did.

History tells us it was Adams who initiated the idea of "Independence" at the First Continental Congress. It was Adams who wrote the Declaration of Rights, spelling out what freedom looked like. It was Adams who penned the first list of National Goals. It was Adams who envisioned the need for a Continental Army. It was Adams who nominated George Washington to serve as Commander-in-Chief. And it was Adams who asked Thomas Jefferson to write the Declaration of Independence. More than anyone, it was Adams who cast the national vision and staffed it with the proper manpower.

Although Great Britain controlled the global economy and possessed the world's greatest war machine, and although America had very little money and no army or navy, and although this war of independence lasted eight long years, ol' King George never had a chance. Because when leadership casts a clear vision and surrounds itself with the right talent, nothing can stop it.

But John Adams was no superhero. His list of shortcomings was at least as long as ours. He was raised in rural anonymity. Soon after his father died. John was shy and battled depression all his life. But his integrity could not be denied. There were many who distrusted him and called him a fanatic. His thin skin left him bruised inside. But the American Revolution could never have happened without John Adams.

Pastors play a similar role for the cause of Christ. Our critics aim their verbal muskets in our direction. Our biblical message is under siege. Our decisions are second-guessed, even by our own recruits. We know all about thin skin. But our work is about the Savior, and the price we pay could never be too high.

So tighten that triangular hat and cinch the belt on those short pants. Cast a big vision and surround yourself with faithful followers. The work of God's kingdom is under attack, and you've been called upon to lead the battle.

20

The Secret of Great Preaching

—ᴍ—

Sermons: the stock and trade for any pastor and every worship service; the exercise by which we're most often evaluated.

Verbiage: an avalanche of needless expression that buries our message; the exercise by which we're most often criticized.

Verbal faux pas: those slips of the tongue that spice an otherwise ordinary Sunday; the items by which we're most often quoted. For example:

- *"Next week's sermon is, What Is Hell? Come early and hear the choir practice."*
- *"Dr. Mohler, a local dentist, will sing, "Crown Him with Many Crowns."*
- *"The Church Unity Service is cancelled due to a conflict."*
- *"GOD IS GOOD, Pastor Miller is better."*
- *"Bertha Belch, our missionary to Africa, will speak at the evening service. Come and hear Bertha Belch all the way from Africa."*

Words: our best friends or our worst enemies.

Each week we step to the pulpit, clear our throats, and launch into our next installment of words—five thousand is the average sermon. Sometimes it's an obvious bull's-eye. Other times it's like Bertha belching all the way from Africa.

What makes for great preaching? Certainly, preaching His Word is the key. "For the Word of God is alive and active. It cuts more keenly than any two edged sword...."

But many churches preach the Word without any apparent impact. Even the Pharisees taught the Word...but wound up obstructing God's work.

So how did Jesus pull it off? What made His sermons the talk of the town? What kept the multitudes spellbound to His every word?

His words were filled with authority. To a nation jaded by a plethora of babbling rabbis, Jesus was unique. Whereas the clergy quoted each other, Jesus quoted God. In fact, He recounted verses from twenty-two of the thirty-nine Old Testament books. He named twenty different OT characters. He spoke on forty biblical themes. The Scriptures were His authority. He used them liberally and they pierced deeply. *"The people were astonished at His teaching."*

His words were filled with creativity. *"Never did a man speak the way this man speaks."* He identified His audience and spoke their language. Whether farmers, tax collectors, harlots, or fishermen, He spoke in a manner they could understand. He established a principle for preaching: The higher the predictability, the lower the impact; the lower the predictability, the higher the impact. His words connected. And the people couldn't get enough of Him. *"They listened to Him with delight."*

His words were filled with integrity. *"In Him was life, and the life was the light of men."* He was His own best message. He lived His words. His holy life removed any doubt about His authenticity. His absence of sin made Him impossible to condemn. Though, in truth, no one was above Him, no one was beneath Him either. His complete humility was in perfect sync with His absolute authority. No one could replicate a godly life more than God Himself.

There's a great line in Jesus' prayer of John 17. *"The words that You gave to Me, I have given to them."* Jesus' words were the Father's words. They're full of power. They revolutionized lives then and now.

Pulpit work is not show biz. It's life and death. It's the light that fights against the darkness. Words won't always flow as beautifully as we'd like but we can still make each of them count.

21

Timeless Rules for Success

—∿—

"How did you become a preacher?" It's a question we've heard thousands of times. The answers differ with year and location but each bottom line is always the same: *"God has chosen the foolish things of this world to confuse the wise, the weak things of this world to confound the strong...."*

Looking for great preachers, it would appear, was never on God's shopping list.

It's ironic that the preacher to whom God gave those words—the apostle Paul—was one of the more prolific preachers of his day. Certainly, if anyone deserved his name in lights it was the rising star from Tarsus.

But *humility*, not headlines, is the staple for the man of God. The Scripture warns us to "Put it on," to "Serve with it," to "Walk in it," to "Be clothed with it," and promises, "Honor comes only after it."

I'm convinced that Paul must have shaken his head in amazement at the concept. That's because his pre-Christian days were probably filled with anything *but* humility. In the fraternity of up-and-coming rabbis he was the blue-chipper, a Pharisee by birth and belief. Studying under the surname of Saul, he glowed as the prized protégé of Professor Gamaliel. Even the church stood in awe, knees knocking at the mention of his notorious name. Paul could have written his own ticket for any job in Judaism.

But when he met Christ on the Damascus Road the rules for success changed. No more could he count on sheer talent and tenacity to get him to the top. A new standard had entered the picture. Paul would need more and more of less and less. God had trumped him.

Three years of training in Arabia—and seven more elsewhere—retooled his thinking. "I am the chief of sinners...the least of all the saints...the least of the apostles...I am nothing." Paul discovered his greatness was not in what he *did* but to whom he belonged.

It's always been that way for God's leaders. Humility is a required course in our schooling. And every graduate has his own personal memoirs. For example:

- For thirteen years Joseph fell in a downward spiral. Being hated by his brothers, left to die in a pit, paraded on the auction block in Egypt, defending his honor against the vile Mrs. Potiphar, and incarcerated for a crime he did not commit seasoned the soon-to-be prime minister as nothing else could.

- For forty years Moses was on the fast track to stardom. As the adopted son of Pharaoh's daughter he had the world on a string. Four decades of uptown living can do that to a guy. But God required forty *more* years of "sweatshop" experience in order to make Moses worthy of his assignment.

- David's meteoric rise in Israel was unprecedented. Giants fell before him. Songs were written about him. He was Israel's MVP...and it sent shockwaves through Saul's palace. For the next eleven years, David was on the run. The darkest caves were his hotel rooms, a group of misfits were his allies, tear-stained psalms were his outlet. And the soft-hearted shepherd became king.

You may be taking a forced march through The Valley right now. But don't panic, God never takes His children to greatness without this detour. It's when we resurface from that valley that God's matured preachers are better equipped to shake a world He loves.

22

Laws That Cannot Be Broken

—⁓—

At first it seems impossible. How can a Boeing 747, weighing nearly one million pounds, ever get off the ground? Nothing that big could suspend itself in air. Feathery birds can fly, but not massive tubes of metal. Nope, it just can't happen. It's impossible. Five hundred tons of shiny steel will never be airborne.

But the truth is it *has* to fly. In fact, it can't do anything *but* fly.

Here's why: When an aircraft moves down a runway the air pressure around the wings changes. The air moving over the rounded surface on the topside of the wing is forced to travel in a curve. As it does, its air speed increases, which causes the air pressure to drop. Meanwhile, on the bottom side of the wing, the air moves in a straight line and, because it's moving slower than the air on top of the wing, the pressure is intensified.

Now, here's where it gets really exciting! Any high-pressure area always moves toward a low-pressure area. Meaning, the underneath-air pushes up on the wings trying to get to the area over the wings. Therefore, the faster the 747 rolls down the runway, the greater the pressure on the bottom of the wings. And the greater the underside-pressure, the more *lift* to the aircraft.

As the jet increases its speed there's more and more pressure pushing on the bottom of the wings. And in moments, bingo! One million pounds of 747 lift off the ground.

What at first appeared impossible becomes an everyday occurrence, because it has to. It's not a miracle, it's simply a physical law designed by the Architect of the Universe.

The role of the church—God's handmade instrument to storm Hell's gates—is not dissimilar to the principle of flight. Everything tells you it's impossible, there's too much opposition, the odds are against us. But, whether your church is a 747 or an Ultralight, divine rules apply. The same great Architect who crafted the universe has also birthed the church. And He's laid out biblical principles that govern her survival and effectiveness.

And yet, at times, it still seems impossible; unmet needs are staggering, the leadership shortage continues, sin abounds, and staff clashes threaten to bring down years of ministry. It all seems to spell doom to His church.

But this Master Builder has issued an iron-clad guarantee: "The gates of Hell will not prevail against it." This is His church, and His promise is irrefutable.

The job of leading His church is daunting to be sure. But the great Architect has purposely placed His handpicked recruits—you and me—to ensure the proper building and maintenance of the body. He's even gifted us with the necessary tools for the work. Nothing will derail His church.

Ours is no ordinary role. No calling in the world is quite like God's call to lead His people. Pastoring is the ultimate life-and-death profession. Our job requirements differ from every other occupation; the demands are intense, the hours are long, and the stakes are high. Tending wayward sheep has never been easy.

But it is doable.

At times our jobs may look impossible. But in every generation frail leaders, just like us, have taken the reins for the task. And, surprisingly, God does the undoable. He uses mortal pastors to accomplish His work. It's not a miracle, it's simply a spiritual law designed by this same Architect.

23

It All Started With Thanksgiving

—ᘶ—

November always brings out the historian in me—undoubtedly a result of those Thanksgiving theatricals at my elementary school. The class would dress as Pilgrims, my broad-brimmed hat stabilized by a pair of crumpled ears. The routines were more funny than factual, but they plowed a furrow of America's history deep into my mind.

And with each November I find myself retracing America's past and always arriving at the same conclusion: America is a miracle, an answer to countless prayers and thankful hearts. There's no other way to explain it.

Don't get me wrong; I don't attribute this nation's greatness solely to the Pilgrims—a name given them by William Bradford, quoting from Hebrews 11:13—even though their prayers, which will always be identified with that original Thanksgiving, certainly played a part.

What makes that first Thanksgiving so memorable is as much about the *when* as it was the *what*. Whereas it's true they had enjoyed a bountiful harvest that year, the Pilgrims purposely planned their Thanksgiving of 1621 during an exceedingly disastrous year. It was *then* that they gave *thanks* to God.

Pull up a chair and grab your almanac. And once you've found that famous Thanksgiving day, see if you notice the change of fortunes for our nation and the beginning of the miracle:

- 1609—Approximately 300 colonists arrived in Jamestown. That winter, because their food supplies were exhausted, 80 percent of the people died from starvation and disease.

- 1620—102 Pilgrims boarded the Mayflower and three months later landed at Plymouth. Within the first year, half of them perished.
- 1621—The Pilgrims dedicated three days for a Thanksgiving Feast to give God glory.
- 1689—During the next 74 years, four North American wars raged between England and France. The final conflict—the French and Indian War—caused Britain to tighten its grip on the colonies, a major miscalculation that eventually led to the American Revolution.
- 1776—America declared independence from England. It was David revisiting Goliath. And, without historical precedent, America won its independence, the world's first colony to break away from a parent country.

It had to be a miracle. Even George Washington thought so: "It will not be believed that such a force as Great Britain, after eight years of military employment, could be so baffled in their plans…by men oftentimes half-starved, almost always sick, without pay, and experiencing every distress which the human nature is capable of enduring."

Yet, soon after the war, four hundred armed war veterans circled the makeshift congressional building demanding their unpaid back wages. Held hostage, Congress was forced to approve a payment plan—but had no funds to make the plan work.

To make matters worse, the thirteen states turned on each other. States they were, but *united* they weren't. New Jersey instituted its own customs services. New York negotiated its own foreign treaties. Nine of the thirteen states maintained their own private navies. Seven states printed their own currency—good only within their borders. Many passed tariff laws against the other states.

And yet somehow these colonies, this people, this collection of war-worn Americans became one nation. A nation ruled by the laws of democracy to safeguard the rights of its citizens—the right to worship as we please, the right to speak boldly about the things of God…

It *was* a miracle. It *is* a grand land. And there's *much* to be thankful for.

24

A Night the World Will Never Forget

It was little ol' Bethlehem, but it was big enough for God. It was quite a contrast trading the throne room of heaven for a stable, angels for cattle, hallelujahs for a lullaby. Bethlehem had its share of visitors, but never one like this.

The prophets had given pieces of the divine puzzle, but even they didn't understand the wonder of *this* event. The Alpha and Omega was born. The Ancient of Days had the skin of a newborn. The same voice that commanded creation into being had the familiar ring of baby-talk.

A child was born of a virgin.

It was a typical Bethlehem night. Dinner was a memory, chores were all done, parents were tucking in their sleepy kids. The stars were out but nothing else. The weary town had said "Goodnight." It was a night like any other, yet it was a night the world will never forget.

Never before had the Eternal become so tiny, the Almighty become so helpless. He had out-muscled Pharaoh's army, but now He was held in Mary's arms. The eyes that see the beginning to the end could hardly open. The God who never slumbers was fast asleep.

Angels were dispatched to spread the word. First stop—a group of shepherds. It was Good News! It was great joy! It was one sentence, only one verse, nineteen small words: "For unto you is born this day in the city of David a Savior, which is Christ the Lord." The announcement needed no explanation, only directions. "You'll find the babe lying in a manger." Finally the wait was over. The Messiah had come. Nothing else mattered, not the late hour, not the restless sheep—nothing. This was a party they couldn't miss, the birthday of the God-child. And yet it was open to lowly shepherds. Fear was replaced by excitement, doubts with hope.

One can only imagine the thoughts of those shepherds as they found the baby-king. There was no entourage, no fanfare. "Where's the red carpet, the music, the royal crib?" There was no need for those things. They would have been out of place. Nothing glitzy could have enhanced the wonder of God becoming flesh. Some appearances don't need an opening act.

There they were. Quiet, perhaps. Motionless, no doubt. They must have thought about Israel's future, or even the dreaded Romans. Someone probably asked to hold the baby. One confused shepherd probably wished he had paid attention in Sabbath school. Another may have remembered the prophet's words, "For unto us a child is born, unto us a son is given; and the government will be upon His shoulders; and His name shall be called Wonderful, Counselor, The Mighty God, The Everlasting Father, The Prince of Peace."

Did they see the irony? They had been watching Bethlehem's sheep, yet now they were beholding the Lamb of God. For years they had supplied animals for the annual sacrifice. But at this moment God had supplied the eternal sacrifice for the sins of the world. Their business was in jeopardy, but their salvation was secure.

These eyewitnesses studied every detail and memorized every word. For years they must have told and retold the accounts.

No, Bethlehem had never seen a visitor like that before—nor since, for that matter. As God often does, He used a nondescript location to change the world, a typical night to revolutionize time, a band of nameless shepherds to tell the world "all they had seen and heard."

25

Innovative Thinking

—◊◊◊—

His friends called him Hitch. His mother called him Alfred. Hollywood called him genius.

For fifty years Alfred Hitchcock served as the dean of movie makers, virtually rewriting the filmmaking rules. No one created suspense or subtext quite like him. For example, he dared to film the most memorable scene of *North by Northwest* without dialog or background music. His unique camera angles made *Psycho* the icon of chiller flicks.

For two generations Alfred Hitchcock was the maestro of mystery, the Caesar of cinema. He was the biggest box office attraction of his day. Even more than the young beauties who starred in his films.

But, like all mortal gods, Hitchcock ultimately met his match: Boredom was his dreaded foe. His director's chair had become all too familiar. The job was mundane and monotonous, just another day on the rock pile.

In an effort to rekindle his passion, Hitchcock devised an innovative plan to jump-start his movie-making enthusiasm: cameo appearances. His cameos became a game. Where would the famed director hide his mug-shot next? It was an early version of Where's Waldo. If you're in search mode, here's where to look:

- In *The Birds* he's found walking past a pet shop with two white terriers as Tippi Hedren appears.
- In *North by Northwest* he's spotted missing a bus during the opening credits.
- In *Psycho* he's seen through Janet Leigh's window wearing a cowboy hat.

- In *Rear Window* he's winding a clock in the neighbor's apartment.
- In *Dial M for Murder* he's seen in Ray Milland's class reunion photo.
- In *Shadow of a Doubt* he's playing cards on a train. He has the entire suit of spades in his hand.
- In *Topaz* he's being pushed through an airport in a wheelchair. Hitchcock then stands up, shakes hands with a man, and walks off.
- In *Lifeboat* he was faced with his most difficult assignment: how to create a cameo when the entire film takes place in a nine-person raft.

Innovation is the oxygen for the suffocating 9-to-5 routine. The straight line of conformity is poison to the power of imagination. Innovative backroads, though often more winding, are far less congested and oh so refreshing.

Over the centuries, the people of God have been criticized for their lack of innovation. We're better known for our traditions than we are for our ideas. In a world of pigeons, we're considered statues. But the truth is we come from a long line of innovators:

- Noah, the shipbuilder, used his large barge as a visual aid to proclaim the gospel.
- Ol' Abraham saw plenty of innovation while bouncing baby Isaac on his knee.
- Joshua's ringing of Jericho was not a normal battle strategy.
- Solomon's Temple was a one-of-a-kind.
- Jehoshaphat's choir-led army raised more than a few eyebrows.
- Jeremiah's sermons never consisted of three points and a poem.
- John the Baptist's wardrobe still hasn't caught on.

No, the spokesmen of God have never been ordinary.

Throughout Scripture, whenever God empowered His leadership team, it was always characterized by innovation, never status quo.

Innovative thinking has always been a hallmark of God's leaders. It's what keeps us fresh and engaging. It was for that reason that Paul told Timothy, "Stir up that inner fire which God gave you." Regain that passion. Turn the mixer to *whip*, and watch things happen.

P.S. If you knew that *Lifeboat's* cameo shows Hitchcock in a newspaper weight loss ad being carried by a passenger, you're spending far too much time at the video store.

26

Public Opinion vs. Godly Obedience

— ∿ —

Few biblical characters compare with King Saul, the tall, dark, and handsome leader of Israel. And what a resume! He was chosen by God, commissioned by Samuel, confirmed by a military victory, and cheered by an adoring public over whom he reigned for forty years as the nation's first monarch. But in the end, "He was afraid, and his heart trembled greatly. And when Saul inquired of the Lord, the Lord did not answer him."

Poor, pathetic, hopeless Saul.

How does a guy fall from a divinely appointed penthouse to a self-imposed outhouse so quickly? Samuel knew: "You did not obey the Lord!"

Godly leadership has less to do with public opinion and everything to do with obedience to God. In the final analysis, obedience covers a multitude of leadership weaknesses. That's because obedience to the Almighty always produces confidence while disobedience always produces fear.

Opposition was the proving ground for Saul. It's the same for any leader. Testing showcases our belief system. We either wait upon the Lord or go forward in our own strength. Saul chose the latter. He saw the overwhelming odds against him, became impatient for God's answer, and took matters into his own hands. And he flopped. His fear was conceived at the union of impatience and self-reliance.

Even today opposition can bear ugly children. And their intimidation has paralyzing effects. Not everyone can deal with it. But those who "stand firm" and "wait upon the Lord" will learn lessons taught in no other classroom. For example:

- Joseph spent thirteen years between his brothers' betrayal and when God elevated him to prime minister. During *that* time he learned the Almighty's sufficiency.
- For forty years Moses sat under the finest teachers in the world. But not until he was tutored in the backside of the desert did he learn how to lead effectively.
- David was in exile for eleven years because a jealous king saw him as competition. But during *those* years David became the servant leader that revolutionized a nation.

Mark Twain said, "A man who carries a cat by the tail will learn something he can learn in no other way." Joseph, Moses, and David were all great leaders *because* of the claw marks.

Successful cat-carriers are rare. Leadership has never been easy.

It's no wonder that God was forever encouraging those whom He picked as leaders: "Be strong; be courageous, be careful." In fact, He specifically told His finest, "Do not be afraid!" Why? Because, they were!

- God told Abraham, "Do not be afraid."
- God told Isaac, "Do not be afraid."
- God told Jacob, "Do not be afraid."
- God told Moses—on three different occasions—"Do not be afraid."
- Three times God told Joshua, "Do not be afraid."
- On ten occasions Jesus told His disciples, "Do not be afraid."
- Twice God told Paul, "Do not be afraid."

And the list goes on and on.

Shepherding is a skilled occupation. It isn't for everyone because worrisome sheep can be exasperating. If the shepherd runs, so will the sheep. The best of sheepherders wear a fleece jacket to—in the minds of the sheep—become one of them. And during the long, cold nights the sheep will sleep because the faithful shepherd watches over them.

That's how the Good Shepherd does it for us, and that's how we do it for His flock.

27

The Greatest Story Ever Told

—w—

It's the mother-lode of Scripture, the Hope Diamond of truth. It's Fort Knox in a book. And every week we're asked to stand in front of a congregation and display its dazzling beauty: "I have loved you with a love that lasts forever, and with unfailing love I've drawn you to myself."

It's the story of God's immeasurable heart and incomparable love, offered without strings and paid in full to an undeserving and resistant people. No one could have devised such a plan—no one except God. It's so…like Him!

During the early years of his ministry, Dwight L. Moody was visiting churches in England when he met a young and eager preacher named Henry Moorhouse. Moody, in a polite but insincere gesture, invited Moorhouse to visit him: "If you should ever get to Chicago, come preach in my church." It was a glib comment. Moody never intended to surrender his pulpit to the Brit.

A month after Moody returned home, he got a telegram from Moorhouse: "Have just arrived in New York. Will be in Chicago on Sunday."

Moody was dumbfounded and embarrassed. And, to make matters worse, he was scheduled to be elsewhere that same Sunday. Yet he had made a promise.

Moody explained the situation to his church leaders and instructed them to allow Moorhouse "to preach one time. If the people enjoy him, put him on again."

A week later Moody returned from his trip. He inquired of his wife how the young Moorhouse had fared. "He was wonderful," she replied. "He's even better than you are. He told sinners that God loves them!"

"But that's wrong," Moody complained. "God does not love sinners!"

"Then you better go tell him yourself," she said, "because he's convinced that God does."

"You mean he's still here?" asked Moody.

"Yes," she said, "and he's been preaching every night since you left."

That evening, Moody went to the meeting and heard Moorhouse preach on *The Unconditional Love of God.* It was Moorhouse's sixth consecutive night in Moody's pulpit, and all six sermons were based upon the same text: "For God so loved the world…."

Moody was spellbound. For the first time he had been confronted with the enormity of God's grace and the openness of His love. Moody's life and ministry were never again the same.

Fifty years later, songwriter Frederick Lehman was moved by the same truth. After reading and rereading "I have loved you with an everlasting love," Lehman wrote:

> *The love of God is greater far than tongue or pen can ever tell,*
> *It goes beyond the highest star and reaches to the lowest hell.*
> *O love of God, how rich and pure! How measureless and strong!*
> *It shall for evermore endure the saints and angels' song.*

Oddly, the hymn's third verse was written by a man the composer never met, Ben Isaac Nahorai. The unknown Nahorai had suffered for years from mental depression and was finally committed to an asylum. While there he too discovered the immense love of God. After Nahorai's death these words were found written on his asylum wall:

> *Could we with ink the ocean fill and were the skies of parchment made,*
> *Were every stalk on earth a quill and every man a scribe by trade,*
> *To write the love of God above would drain the ocean dry,*
> *Nor could the scroll contain the whole, tho' stretched from sky to sky.*

The story of God's immeasurable love is what we've been chosen to tell. It's God's gift to mankind, and our privilege to deliver.

28

The Gospel According to Attila the Hun

—⁘—

For centuries the resilient Roman Empire withstood every attack from history's most formidable foes. Through it all the proud empire never wavered. But then, out of the steppes of Central Asia, came an invasion of unorthodox, nomadic tribes throwing Rome into disarray and ultimately to its ruin. The Huns had arrived.

Growing up a Hun wasn't your typical childhood. Their favorite toy was a noose; their favorite game was fisticuffs. The 3-Rs were Rob, Ransack, and Rebel. Their patron saint was Bluebeard. The Hun credo was:

- If I like it, it's mine.
- If I think it's mine, it's mine.
- If I can take it from you, it's mine.

Being king of the Huns was a specialty. Each rose to leadership via the survival-of-the-fittest mode. If you wanted the job badly enough, and a rival didn't assassinate you before you could assassinate him, you got the job.

Historians agree that the most famous Hun king was Attila. Under his barbaric leadership southern Europe became his stomping ground. His thrill for conquest wowed the half-million Hun troops. Together they ate raw meat, slept on horseback, and destroyed city after city. Their post-conquest drinking parties are historic.

Attila was Europe's public enemy No. 1. The Romans called him the "Scourge of God."

But history is split on labeling this man. Some historians have lionized him as a great and noble king. After all, Attila was able to unite uneducated masses from primitive lands into one nation. He cast the vision. He led the charge. He set the standard. And—recognizing that Rome was ready to collapse—Attila believed his time had arrived.

Now switch gears. Leave the fifth century and return to the twenty-first.

From our cultured mindset, it's difficult to see any redeeming value in this barbaric bully and his hordes of hoods. And whereas the Hun nation and our Bible-believing churches have absolutely nothing in common, the similarity between Attila's leadership task and the role of a pastor is uncanny.

In his book *The Leadership Secrets of Attila the Hun*, author Wess Roberts writes:

> The Huns were a nomadic, multiracial, and multilingual conglomeration of people. Attila's task, as King of Huns, was to instill a new sense of morale and discipline that would build unity within these barbaric tribes. The Hun's greatest destiny could only be served when each individual or group would set aside their independent ways and undisciplined thinking. Attila believed that any peace in the Huns camp would result only when the nomads found a new spirit; something to rally around; a cause greater than themselves.

Roberts concluded, "Attila's job was not a simple chore!"

Not a simple chore indeed! Ask any pastor who's been commissioned by God to mobilize a nomadic, multiracial, multilingual, multigenerational conglomeration of people and you'll hear the same story. It's NOT easy!

But Attila's plan was backwards: He thought peace was a byproduct of unity.

The truth is, unity is a byproduct of peace—with God. Jesus made that very clear:

- "Holy Father, keep them in Thy name...that they may be one, even as We are."

- "Sanctify them in the truth…that they may all be one."
- "I in them, and Thou in Me, that they may be perfected in unity."

Unity only comes when we're united with the Prince of Peace and sanctified by His truth.

It's no wonder the Huns didn't last long after the death of their great king. As Attila's sons fought for control, their father's empire became divided. Soon all those who hated the Huns used this opportunity to rebel against Hun rule. Finally, the empire fell and disappeared from history.

Maybe Attila the Hun has something to teach us after all.

29

Bumpy Roads and Beautiful Endings

—∿—

"Are we there yet?" Ah, the familiar sound of a weary traveler. Whether it's the distance, hazards, or just boring scenery, some journeys are longer than others. Maybe you're on one of those unenviable journeys right now. It's easy to tell—every time you look ahead, there's bumpy road as far as the eye can see.

Job's life was a journey. Even when he asked for directions all he got was road conditions. His travel consultant, Eliphaz, lamented, "Man is born for trouble." It was the naysayer's way of saying, "You can't get there from here!"

Abraham's life was a journey. Just when his wheels pulled out of the deep ruts, he hit potholes. He'd waited twenty-five years for God's promise—and then was told to sacrifice it.

Jesus probably had these journeys in mind when He said, "No one who puts his hand to the plow—and then looks back—is fit for service in the kingdom of God." Bumpy roads—fender-rattling, bone-jarring, coffee-spilling bumps—come with the territory.

Long, hard journeys appear to be part of life's DNA. In fact, God's creation points to it:

- The gray whale navigates 10,000 miles up and down the West Coast each year at a speed comparable to a child on a bicycle… because he has to.
- Every year the Arctic tern is required to relocate 22,000 miles away, roughly the circumference of the earth.
- Desert locusts have been known to cross oceans for a preprogrammed raid.

- The ever-so-slow leatherback turtle must travel 3,000 miles annually for his favorite meal: jellyfish a la carte.
- The Monarch butterfly, which can't even fly a straight line and is forever losing momentum to the gentlest breeze, is compelled to migrate 3,000 miles, a trek that takes five *generations* to complete.

No, some journeys seem to be incredibly long.

I'm always impressed by fellow travelers who've "fought the good fight" and "finished the course," who didn't "grow weary in well doing," who "[ran] with endurance the race set before [them]," even though their long journeys were often very lonely.

Men like:

- Charles Simeon. For fifty-four years he pastored Holy Trinity Church at Cambridge. During that journey he endured isolation, boycotts, locked doors, pews thrown into the streets, slander, obscenities, rotten egg barrages, and riots—all because of his faithful, biblical teaching in a secular culture.
- Andrew Murray. At age twenty-one, Murray began a sixty-eight-year pastorate that covered fifty thousand square miles of dangerous terrain. His passion for the African people was seen through his many evangelistic tours and deep involvement in tribal education. He bitterly opposed the growing apartheid movement and its contemporary label as "Christian."
- Dietrich Bonhoeffer. While millions were slaughtered, the German church leaders remained silent, fearful that speaking out might "cause the reputation of the church to suffer." Bonhoeffer fought back. "When Christ calls a man, He bids him come and die." As Bonhoeffer's journey gained worldwide recognition, the Lutheran pastor was executed in a Nazi concentration camp.

Paul was very familiar with these long, brutal roads. In fact he visited them often. But rather than hating them, he looked for Christ while traveling on them, "That I may know Him...and the fellowship of His sufferings, being conformed to His death."

Be encouraged. Tough roads lead to places you'll be glad you visited. Don't give up. Don't quit. "Don't get discouraged, for we will reap a harvest of blessing at the appropriate time."

30

The State of the Union, circa 1775

—⁓⁓—

The short list of candidates had been narrowed to one finalist. He was tall and handsome, articulate and experienced. His resume was impressive, his character flawless. Yet, with all that pedigree, the odds of his success were almost nil.

Nevertheless, on June 15, 1775, John Adams stood to his feet during the Second Continental Congress and nominated George Washington of Virginia to be Commander in Chief of the Continental Army.

In retrospect, hiring the forty-three-year-old former soldier and surveyor was the most important decision of the American Revolution.

Prior to Washington's acceptance speech, Congress gushed about the "large and high-spirited army" and how they would "provide any and all resources necessary." They intentionally misrepresented the facts for fear that Washington would be scared off by the impossibility of the task.

Soon after his humble acceptance, where he declined their monthly salary of $500 in favor of expenses only, Washington discovered the ugly truth about the state of the union. The army's head-count was almost half of what he'd been promised. Furthermore, there wasn't enough food, supplies, pay, guns, or ammunition to go around. And, to make matters worse, the enlistment period for most of the soldiers was about to expire.

General Washington's mammoth task was to: 1) motivate thousands of cold, unpaid, overworked, underfed, retiring veterans to re-enlist for more of the same; and 2) defeat the well-equipped, expertly trained war machine of Great Britain. That's all.

To accomplish these goals, Washington committed himself to a four-point strategy:

1.) ***To surround himself with young, vibrant officers*** who could replicate his leadership on multiple battlefields.
2.) ***To demand military discipline***. Most enlistees viewed military service as a secondary job and, as a result, were halfhearted about their responsibilities.
3.) ***To teach his troops about freedom***. In every briefing he spoke of tyranny and liberty and history in the making. He read and reread the *Declaration of Independence* to them. Each day he reminded them that they were fighting to be free.
4.) ***To offer himself as an example***. He would not ask others to sacrifice unless he was willing to do the same. Consequently, during one battle, four bullets ripped through his coat and his horse was shot out from under him. In others, he stayed on horseback for days at a time, riding from one flank to the next, encouraging the men.

In time, the American Revolution was won, a nation was founded, and a national hero was born.

Washington's leadership plan, whether he knew it or not, was biblically based. In fact it's the identical strategy that God has given to us as we lead His church:

1.) "***Commit [your teaching] to faithful men*** who will be able to teach others also" (2 Tim 2.2).
2.) "***Be serious and watchful***...and above all things have fervent love for one another" (1 Pet. 4.7-8).
3.) "***Walk in a manner worthy of God who calls you*** into His own kingdom and glory" (1 Thess. 2.12).
4.) "***Be an example to the believers*** in speech, in conduct, in love, in faith, in purity" (1 Tim. 4:12).

A general and a pastor have very similar roles. Both are highly visible and yet can be very lonely. Both hear the applause of adoring troops and yet feel the pain of well-aimed bullets. Their leadership determines the destiny of lives. Generals change history. So do pastors—one life at a time.

31

Time Tellers and Clock Builders

—⚎—

Anyone can tell time, but only a few build clocks. Augustus Pugin was a clock builder.

After the famed Palace of Westminster burned to the ground in 1834, Sir Charles Berry was commissioned to rebuild the central piece of London's famed skyline. The new palace—known today as the House of Parliament—would be fashioned in Victorian Gothic architecture crowned by a skyward tower showcasing the world's largest clock.

But clock building is a specialty—especially a clock measuring 23 feet in diameter, spinning a 9-foot hour hand and 14-foot minute hand while supporting a 14-ton bell. Moreover, the four-sided timepiece would have to synchronize with precise accuracy high above the gazing Londoners who wished to tell *correct* time. That's where Augustus Pugin came in. Pugin built clocks.

It appears the world consists of two types of people: time tellers and clock builders.

Time tellers don't care about details; they just want to know what time it is. Theirs is a world of status quo. They live life as it comes—minute by minute, hour by hour. They're satisfied to watch time fly by. But clock builders think differently. They march to the beat of a different chime; they hear the distant tick, tick, tick of *what if?* And that enticing ticking is the lure that clock builders can't ignore.

In business they're called "chiefs." On Wall Street they're "bulls." On Capitol Hill they're "whips." They're the ones who challenge the status quo, who turn up the volume, who bite and swallow at the same time. They're cut from new cloth. They sleep and eat less but dream and do more. They swim in the deep end. Their socks don't match because they don't put them on at the same time.

They see the world skewed and then they put it right:

- Noah's building project drew plenty of skeptics who could neither build clocks nor tell time.
- Twelve spies entered the Promised Land. When they returned, ten gave the time while Caleb and Joshua built clocks.
- As Nehemiah rebuilt Jerusalem's wall he was mocked by the local time tellers.
- Martha was busy telling time while Mary quietly built a clock.
- Esau, Barak, King Saul, and Ananias all mastered the art of time telling, while Jacob, Deborah, David, and Stephen built clocks.

Clock builders are always characterized by passion and risk. These two forces separate the day-dreamers from the day-makers. "Business as usual" is never found in their vocabulary. They say things like, "Has anyone ever tried..." or, "There must be another way!"

But as refreshing as clock builders are, they rarely hear cheers. In fact, they're usually forced to go it alone:

- Seventeen-year-old Joan of Arc was determined to right the human injustices in France. When asked, "What if no one follows you?" she answered, "I'll never notice because I won't look back."
- In 1889, Rudyard Kipling, an aspiring writer, was sent a rejection notice from the editor of the *San Francisco Examiner*: "I'm sorry, Mr. Kipling, but you don't know how to use the English language."
- In 1901, critic Harry Thurston Peck wrote of Mark Twain, "Nothing this man writes will be remembered 100 years from now."
- A leery Hollywood producer witnessed young Fred Astaire's first screen-test. He wrote, "Can't act, can't sing, can dance a little." But he failed to notice that the skinny hoofer built clocks.

Passion—it's what the great ones have. Risk—it's what the successful ones take. Quit—it's the one thing clock builders just can't get the hang of.

32

Stress: The Ecclesiastical Toxin

—ɯ—

In a well-lit corner of my office hangs a hand-sketched sign, cryptic in nature, but oh so familiar to those in our work. By placing the sign where I have, it conveniently appears just over the head of anyone who sits across from my desk.

> *Stress:*
> *That confusion created when one's mind*
> *Overrides the body's desire*
> *To choke the living daylights out of some jerk*
> *Who desperately needs it.*

We're all familiar with stress. It's that jarring pothole that, when hit, sends reverberating shockwaves throughout, often derailing the wheels of ministry.

In an effort to forewarn my fraternity, I'm offering the following Pastor's Stress Test to determine the depth of your pothole.

1. Do you have Dial-a-prayer on speed dial?
2. Is your congregation confused because you're preaching through clinched teeth?
3. Does your personal communion consist of *the bread, the cup,* and two Tums?
4. Does your sermon prep include a yoga class?
5. Have your staff members arranged their schedules to work on your day off?

6. Have you mistakenly used your resignation-in-waiting as a bulletin insert?

A "yes" to any of these questions might indicate a problem.

Despite its public persona, pastoring is filled with stress. It's an ecclesiastical toxin that saps your strength; a stubborn pimple on the face of the church; a mental battering ram that beats on your office door. At times it's the enemy standing on the other side, but sometimes it's your sheep. Either way, it's a workplace staple and the single biggest drain to a pastor's personal joy.

But dealing with stress may produce the greatest sermon we ever *live*. Want proof?

- Ask Moses. His forty years in the wilderness was a constant battle against popular opinion. Never should a leader have to endure his load. Yet Scripture labels him "the most humble man on the face of the earth."
- Ask Samuel. He had the unenviable job of cleaning up the priesthood corruption brought on by his mentor's reprobate sons. Yet Scripture says, "The Lord let none of Samuel's words fail."
- Ask Hosea. His home-life was a train wreck. Dishonored by his wayward, runaway bride, he bought her back at a local slave auction. And together they became a biblical metaphor of God's unquenchable love for His people.
- Ask Habakkuk. His faithful service to a rebellious nation seemed fruitless. In frustration he demanded answers from God. Then God responded. And with that Habakkuk's complaints turned into worship.
- Ask Jonah. Though he was a prophet of God, he had no heart for saving Nineveh. Those deplorable Ninevites deserved the wrath of God! But when this reluctant prophet obeyed God, the largest city in the ancient world was saved.
- Ask Paul. Whereas he was a great church planter, he was also a real troublemaker, causing riots in at least ten cities. And though he usually faced his accusers alone, he declared, "The Lord stood with me, and strengthened me."

A quick scan of Jesus' ministry reveals His own timeless stress management technique: His goal was the finish line, not the hurdles. He ran the race to please the Father, not the grandstand. He used the potholes as venues to do His work. He would not be deterred by the *crisis de jour* ... even if that crisis was a cross. He was focused on one thing: "I have finished the work which You have given me to do."

A mentor of mine, the one who gave me the sign that hangs in my office, also gave me a great stress management verse, Luke 2:1: "And it came to pass..."

Thank God it didn't come to stay.

33

Public Consensus vs.
Personal Conviction

—⁓—

I was intrigued by an article I read in *Preaching Magazine*. I found myself standing up, pacing, reading aloud, making notes, and shouting, "Halle-glory and Praise-elujah." Some things do that to me. This was one of them.

O.S. Hawkins' article took me inside a question that Christ asked His staff. Actually, two questions: one on *Public Consensus* ("Who do **men** say that I am?"), and the other on *Personal Conviction* ("Who do **you** say that I am?").

The questions were posed just outside Caesarea Philippi, Israel's most northern boundary. It was a perfect spot to survey local perceptions of the young evangelist, far from the canned bias of the Jewish leaders in metro Jerusalem.

Hawkins' article, however, took on a different slant, contending that these questions reveal the plumb line for today's pulpiteers. The author believes churches showcase two distinct styles of leadership: pastors who lead by public consensus, i.e. taking a congregation "where they *want* to go," and pastors who lead by personal conviction, i.e. taking a congregation "where they *need* to go."

The trend, he points out, has shifted from *leading* people to *following* them.

But let's be honest, bucking the crowd is no picnic:
- Just ask Aaron about his short-lived stint as leader while Moses was away. The multitude wanted to build a golden calf. And

when asked why he complied, Aaron's only defense was, "The people made me do it!"

- Just ask Peter about his spontaneous answers to an inquisitive young girl while Jesus was on trial. Peter's leadership in the upper room was easy; he was with friends. But outside, among the rank and file of unfamiliar faces, he fell apart.

From the opening moments of Pentecost the church was fashioned to be distinct from the world. God designed us that way, to praise *Him*, to please *Him*. Conforming to the world was not His mandate. His bride was never meant to be one of the girls. Scripture underscores this distinction with words like *peculiar* and *transformed* and *unblemished*.

But though we've been called to be "separate," we seem to be terrified of being *different*. We feel the need to popularize the church, to broaden its appeal. Rather than claiming our spiritual birthright, we work overtime to hide the distinction.

But Jesus didn't do it that way:

- Remember the rich young ruler? When this rising star quizzed Jesus about the prequalifications of eternal life, Jesus gave him a list of commandments intended to underscore the impossibility of the task. But the self-righteous young man claimed to be equal to the task. So Jesus raised the bar because He would not offer *easy believism*, even if it meant losing a great prospect.
- Remember the woman at the well? After five minutes with Jesus she ran into town exclaiming, "Come, meet a man who told me everything I've ever done." And when you consider that she was the most despicable person in town, you begin to realize that Jesus didn't sugarcoat His words.

To the Savior, the gospel was not cheap. Yet the multitudes came from far and wide to hear it. That's because the multitudes desperately wanted something the world couldn't offer.

So do our churches.

Few of Jesus' conversations would be considered *church growth* techniques. His words tended to alienate rather than recruit. Posting attendance figures was not important. Nor was the favor of power-brokers.

His favorite audience was the pitiful, the sinner, and the outcast. His goal wasn't to be admired, but to be followed.

That's still true today.

That's why His question speaks specifically to pastors: "Who do **you** say that I am?"

34

Maintaining Focus in a World of Distractions

—〰—

- Focus (fo-kus) noun, [Latin] 1. A focal point. 2. To concentrate. 3. A center of interest or activity. 4. To sharpen or clearly define. 5. The point at which an object is most clearly seen.

To the casual observer Jesus might appear as a spontaneous nomad who dropped miracles as easily as loose coins, a first-century Johnny Appleseed scattering goodness and golden rules like confetti, or a Galilean Don Quixote whose idealism attracted disciples like stray cats.

But nothing could be further from the truth. Jesus was the world's most focused leader, a genius in organizational development and human resources. He specialized in visionary management, the church being exhibit A.

But that was the easy part. After all, He was God!

Yet within that organizational mindset He faced opposition from every side:

- The religious authorities set traps in hopes of discrediting Him. *"The Pharisees argued with Him, testing Him to see if He was from God."*
- His disciples repeatedly tried to rewrite His agenda: *"… Command a bolt of lightning down out of the sky and incinerate them!"*
- His family questioned His loyalties: *"Why have you treated us this way?"*

- Friends with whom He'd grown up *"were deeply offended and refused to believe in Him."*
- Even Satan took his best shot. *"I'll give you all the kingdoms of the world if you will kneel down and worship me."*

So how did Jesus survive the self-serving bombardment of second guessers and jealous rivals? For that matter, how does any leader—*or pastor*—maintain his focus amidst hostile distractions?

First of all, Jesus was determined to do His Father's will. *"My priority is to do the will of Him who sent Me."* Nothing would divert Him from it—not His growing notoriety, or His triumphant debates with religious opponents, or the dinner invitations from upper class nobility, or the public's perception of His political destiny; not even a cross.

He also focused His message. Every dialogue was deliberate. Each conversation was customized. When a crowd gathered, He was ready: *"The words which you gave to me, I have given to them."* His material was fresh and applicable. To the hurting He spoke of hope. At a funeral He spoke of life. To the blind He spoke of light. To the leper He offered His touch. And they loved Him for it.

He knew how—and with whom—to spend His time. *"I have not come to call the righteous, but sinners to repentance."* He gravitated to the hungry and the needy, not the complacent or stagnant. His ministry was one of depth; the breadth just happened. In fact, He hushed some from telling too much. He commanded others to *"tell no one."*

He wasn't intimidated by complaints that His message was *"too hard to understand"* or when the crowds walked out in droves. Neither was He impressed when the big shots stopped by for an audience.

And He was determined to replicate Himself through His disciples. *"As you have sent me into the world, I am sending them into the world."* He chose a dozen followers, each with varying degrees of strengths and weaknesses, from hundreds of candidates. And for three years they heard it all, saw it all, and were deeply involved in His work. Jesus held nothing back, not even His glory. He schooled them in every phase of ministry. They saw Him laugh, weep, teach, pray, rest, serve, answer, and lead. And when it was their turn they were ready.

Jesus was focused. He was on a mission.

Now it's our turn.

35

Cross-baring in a Difficult Pastorate

—᙮᙮᙮—

Charles Simeon was not your typical pastor. Although I wish he were. And his congregation, Holy Trinity Church on the campus of Cambridge University, was not your normal church. And I'm glad it was not.

Zoom in and you'll see what I mean.

Two hundred years ago, Cambridge students were required to attend church and periodically receive the Lord's Supper. Charles Simeon, a 1779 Cambridge freshman, was not a Christian but somehow understood the importance of communion.

To prepare himself, he purchased the only religious book he'd ever heard of: *Whole Duty of Man*. And before long he fell to his knees crying out for God's mercy. It was a true conversion from which Simeon would never recover.

Upon graduation, Simeon, with assistance from his influential father, was ordained and appointed pastor of Holy Trinity Church at Cambridge.

It was Simeon's dream job—but not for long.

It's hard to imagine the isolation for an evangelical pastor in the halls of Cambridge during the late 1700s, just three years after his conversion.

Alone with his newfound faith, he wrote: "I longed to know some spiritual person who had the same views and feelings. I even considered putting an ad into the papers that would read, *'I'm a young clergyman who feels himself an undone sinner. I've looked to Jesus alone for salvation and I desire to live only to make the Savior known. I'm hopeful there is someone out there whose beliefs agree with mine. But after three years I've found none.'"*

To make matters worse:

- The congregation of Holy Trinity didn't want him as their pastor.
- Church members boycotted his services and pew-holders locked their pews.
- To provide seating, Simeon placed benches in the aisles but the wardens threw them out.
- At times the church leaders locked the doors, preventing him from the services.
- Rowdy university students protested Simeon's preaching with obscenities and riots, and Simeon was pelted with rotten eggs as he left church.
- The faculty treated him with contempt. They slandered and ostracized him.

Why all this abuse? Because Simeon faithfully and consistently taught the truth of man's sinfulness and the bountiful forgiveness available in Christ.

But how much can one man take? Even godly pastors have a breaking point!

One day Simeon took a long walk into the woods to offer God his resignation: "I can't take it anymore, Lord! I just can't!" Finding a stump to sit on, he randomly opened his Bible, hoping for divine confirmation. Instead, his Bible fell open to one lone verse, "*They found a man of Cyrene, **Simeon** by name, and forced him to carry Christ's cross.*"

Charles Simeon, an exhausted and defeated pastor, finally saw his situation through different eyes. "*Lord, lay it on me; lay it on me! I will gladly carry the cross for Your sake.*"

Gradually the tide turned. Growing numbers of students, impressed by his courage, came to hear him speak. Pew-holders, amazed at his determination, reopened their pews. Fellow professors, curious about his tenacity and intellect, came to learn and admire.

For fifty-four years he remained pastor of Holy Trinity Church.

Finally, at age seventy-seven, Simeon was called into God's presence. He had become so loved that when he died all shops in Cambridge closed, university lectures were suspended, and mourners lined four-deep all around the college, waiting to pay their final tribute to their faithful pastor.

Some pastorates are more difficult than others. Yours may be one of them. But, like Simeon, be willing to carry the cross for Christ's sake.

36

A Light Like No Other

—ᴍ—

Light is the oldest member of the universe, having been called into being on day one. Those in the know tell us that light—*real light*—is rarely seen. And yet, ironically, none of us can see without it.

Researchers are baffled by light; they can't even agree on how it works. Is it a wave? A particle? And, whereas they've sliced and diced every known molecule, they can't reduce light. That's because light has no volume.

Confused yet? You're not alone.

No one can define light, either. When asked by his students to explain the phenomenon of light, Aristotle just shook his head and said, "It's the activity of what is transparent."

Say what!?

Plato, ever the innovator, taught his "Fire of the Eye" theory, arguing that, in some strange way, the eye originates its own light. When asked, "Why then can't we see in the dark?" he confessed his theory had a flaw or two.

Over the years light has been a focal point of scientific breakthroughs:

- Albert Einstein based his Theory of Relativity upon the principles of light.
- Science discovered how to keep light from spreading out—as it does naturally—and mold it into a true straight line. They called the process Light Amplification by Stimulated Emission of Radiation. We call it *laser*.

- NASA used light and mirrors to measure the 225,000-mile distance to the moon within a half-inch.
- Soon, it's theorized, a single fiber optic (a transmission via light) will be able to put every person on earth on one phone call simultaneously.
- The Luxor Hotel in Las Vegas created "The World's Brightest Light," a 40-billion candlepower beam aimed straight into the night sky. The illumination is so powerful that you can read a book by its light 10 miles above the earth.
- One enterprising scientist discovered how to make light travel faster than the speed of...*light*.
- And medical research determined that one-fifth of the brain does nothing but deal with light.

All this, and still no one can explain what light is.

Ironically, there's another Light that's also unknown to mankind: the Light of the World.

Seven centuries before Bethlehem's biggest event, God told Isaiah that a Messiah would come "as a light...to bring salvation to the world."

Time passed and the world waited. For centuries the darkness prevailed.

"And it came about that while [Mary and Joseph] were [in Bethlehem] the days were completed for her to give birth...and she gave birth to her firstborn son. And she wrapped Him in cloths and laid Him in a manger."

And the Light was born.

It was history's greatest moment; the Father of Lights gave the world a close-up view of Himself. "I have come as light into the world that everyone who believes in Me will not remain in darkness." With eyes wide open we're able to look directly into that Light and see God, "with whom there is no shadow."

Lowly shepherds came and saw the Light. Wise men saw the same Light. Over the centuries kings and peasants have gazed into His Light, and their eyes were opened.

Lovers of darkness have also looked into the Light, wondering, guessing, and ultimately covering their eyes to hide from its brilliance.

They've run from the Light, but they could never darken it. That's because "His greatness is unreachable and His ways are unfathomable."

The Light of the World has been born! And the story is ours to tell.

37

Preaching—the Centerpiece
of Pastoring

—〜〜—

Will any of us ever forget our first sermon? As hard as I've tried, I can't. It was titled "Called to Abundant Labors." Obviously the title was assigned. In fact, the whole idea was cooked up by the cruel busybodies on the Christian Education Committee. They thought it would be great sport if a couple of ministry-minded teenagers would preach on a Sunday night. You know—a church's version of *American Idol*.

The evening service opened as they always did, a little singing, boring announcements, an offering, and then it was our turn. The other guy spoke first. At fourteen, we were the same age and, I assumed, of equal talent. I was wrong.

He started smoothly, opening with a little joke. I feigned a laugh. He gestured confidently. The crowd seemed impressed. His three points were alliterated. He was quickly getting on my nerves. He quoted Scripture from memory followed by the pastor's loud "Amen!" My *competition* was on a roll. *Please, God, make him stop!* When he finished, the place cheered.

Then it was my turn. Stepping to the microphone felt ominously like walking the plank. I was too nauseous to be nervous. One final adjustment to my clip-on tie caused it to plop into the standing glass of water, spilling onto my handwritten notes, making the ink run. My sermon notes now looked like finger paintings. The crowd began to giggle. My knees weren't knocking, they were missing. I had no joke, no outline, no rhyme or reason.

Twelve minutes later I was done. The church was besieged in cold-sweats. My mother took her first breath. The pastor cringed. The angels wept. It was the worst night of my life.

And God said, "Get used to it, kid, I've called you to preach." And suddenly the words "He uses the foolish things of this world…" had a whole new meaning. Balaam's donkey looked awfully familiar.

Preaching is the centerpiece of pastoring, the non-negotiable in the job description. It serves as the main entree at every worship service, evokes the highest compliments and fuels the hottest critiques. It's how we're defined.

Debates rage over what constitutes a great sermon. Is it cleaver oratory? Is it crowd-pleasing analogies? Is it demonstrative passion? Or is it the congregation's response?

According to Scripture, great preaching has little to do with the size of our talent and everything to do with the size of our God, Peter at Pentecost being proof positive. Proclaiming God's Word was never meant to be show-and-tell for a man and his gift. Great preaching is simply the spoken word opening the written Word to proclaim the incarnate Word.

A head count in the prayer room isn't a success barometer either. Otherwise Hudson Taylor was a flop and William Carey bombed. Nor is a long sermon necessarily a great sermon. Jonah's preaching led to a national revival, although it contained only eight words. For that audience, eight was enough. "Yet forty days and Nineveh shall be overthrown."

In a single prayer, Jesus gave us the clue to His preaching: "I have given them Thy words." When He stood in the pulpit there was no rhetorical fluff. His preaching was biblical, theological, and oh so practical. In a nutshell, it was simple but rich, of God but for man.

"And the multitudes loved listening to Him."

Preaching is a powerful gift of God. Use it carefully.

38

Follow the Leader

—◊—

Look closely and you'll notice a strong similarity between pastoring a church and presiding over a country. Both require a strong vision…and blinders; wisdom…and thick skin; diplomacy…and a willingness to go it alone.

Truth is there aren't many who can do either job—pastor or president. And those who can tend to surprise us all.

For example, no one could have guessed the success of Abraham Lincoln. If ever someone lacked curb appeal, it was the tall-drink-of-water from Illinois. If Springfield High had a Geek Club, he was the chairman. His arms and feet had outgrown his long, lanky body. His hands were the size of dinner plates. His wrinkled and outdated clothes didn't fit. He was corny and common.

And yet he became our sixteenth president.

But even his presidency seemed doomed. Within days of taking office:

- His predecessor, James Buchanan, openly declared that Lincoln would destroy the nation.
- Seven states seceded from the Union.
- The U.S. House of Representatives refused Lincoln's plea to enlarge the military.
- The Senate passed a resolution demanding the War Department reduce military spending.
- Rumors ran rampant that Lincoln would be shot at his inauguration and Washington D.C. would be burned to the ground.

And you thought *your first pastorate* was tough.

To make matters worse the New York and Washington papers viciously attacked him. Their poisoned pens called Lincoln *"a third rate country lawyer, a dictator, an ape, a buffoon."*

Like a left-handed pastor in a right-handed church, Lincoln did not fit the political mold. But America didn't need another politician, it needed a leader. A hot-air filibuster was not the answer. America needed a remedy that placebo politics couldn't cure.

Of all Lincoln's strengths, none were as noticeable as his ability to pick the right people to accomplish his goals. It wasn't important that they agreed with him on all points—only the ones they were responsible for.

First he had to find someone to take command of the Union Army. Candidates would be graded on results, not rank. Military tenure would be superseded by performance. Lincoln wanted someone who believed risk and destiny were synonyms. It took three years and ten generals before he found Ulysses S. Grant, but once he did victory was imminent.

Building a winning team is a science. The key ingredients are *example* and *vision*. The payoff comes when we *empower* and *send*. A room filled with nodding heads won't guarantee success. It's only when we display our passion mixed with shoe leather that those in training learn to serve.

Scripture is filled with those who caught the leader's vision and then followed suit:

- Joshua, when given his turn, knew exactly what to do. He followed Moses' instructions to the letter of the Law.
- 300 unarmed warriors had confidence in Gideon and his God—and terrorized an army of 135,000.
- Without a hiccup Elisha continued the ministry of his departed mentor, Elijah.
- David's mighty men risked their lives just to offer their leader a drink of water.
- Jesus sent His followers and they, in turn, revolutionized the world.

- Peter and John defied the religious and civil leaders who wanted to silence the gospel. Soon all the apostles were doing the same.
- Underachieving Timothy became valuable to the church only after Paul's words, "Do the things you've seen me do."

Ministry's greatest reward is to see others loving and serving the Savior just as we do. It never gets old. Enjoy every moment of it.

39

Famous Last Words

—w—

We all have heard or read "Famous Last Words"—those historic faux pas that outlive their authors, embarrassing memos that rise up to haunt us, impassioned goofs that return like a well-thrown boomerang... Oh, for the ability to erase them all.

Daniel Webster was one of America's greatest living treasures during the early 1800s. His verbal skills, mixed with an extraordinary intellect, positioned him as the most dominant player in American politics. He was without peer. But in 1848, speaking to the U.S. Senate, Webster said something that today makes us smile: "I have never heard of anything more ridiculous, more absurd than the claim that the nation will profit by the acquisition of California. I contend it is not worth one dollar."

Decca Records controlled the American music industry for decades. Their star-filled vault held the contracts of Judy Garland, Bing Crosby, Louis Armstrong, Peggy Lee, Buddy Holly, and many others. Their ear for talent was unmatched. But in 1962, after their talent scouts reviewed a group of "mop heads" from Liverpool called The Beatles, Decca Records said, "We don't like their sound. And besides, guitar music is on the way out." Ten years later, the Decca Records label disappeared.

Economist Irving Fisher, in October 1929, reported that "...the stock market has reached what looks like a permanently high plateau. The market is a safe and prudent investment." That same month, a deafening thud was heard throughout America as Wall Street crashed.

In 1942, Thomas J. Watson, chairman of IBM, said, "Realistically, there is a market for about five computers in the entire world. There is no reason to risk our current success on such a limited venture."

Looking into the future and reading the trends accurately is a rare ability.

You'd expect the apostle Paul, one of history's most quoted personalities, to have left a memorable line or two among his *last words*. After all, during his ministry he'd been offered a preview into the future. Through a God-given knothole, Paul peeked into heaven's splendor. Surely his last words would include something about golden streets and pearly gates. But instead, Paul's farewell was not about the *then-and-there* but rather the *here-and-now*. He spoke, of all things, about pastoring.

Paul's final words were addressed to Timothy, a pastoral candidate. Like many ministerial plebes, Timothy had questioned this strange choice of occupation. His mentor had more scars than friends, more jail time than spare time. And because Paul's battles were from both sides of the church door, Timothy must have wondered, "How can anyone shepherd unruly sheep and menacing wolves at the same time?"

The apostle didn't leave his protégé wondering for long. Paul's exhortation has become his *famous last words*:

- Be faithful in your duties (2 Tim. 1:8)
- Hold on to sound doctrine (2 Tim. 1:13)
- Guard what you say and do (2 Tim. 2:22-24)
- Be willing to suffer persecution for the gospel (2 Tim. 3:12)
- Work hard at preaching the Word (2 Tim. 4:1-2)

These were Paul's non-negotiable pastoral priorities. That's why he could say, "I've fought the good fight, I've finished the course, I've kept the faith."

And, as a result, Paul—and countless others like him—heard another set of famous last words: *"Well done, thou good and faithful servant…enter into the joy of your master."* Is that your goal too?

40

Strong Medicine Never Tastes Good

—∿—

Jeremiah would have made a great radio broadcaster. His program would certainly generate a lot of negative mail, but it would be worth it. More than any other Old Testament prophet, his unpopular messages served as Judah's emergency broadcast system. But even though his warnings were designed for national security, many in that day wished he would just shut up!

Jerusalem's church crowd resented his sermons, but they wouldn't have missed one. They tuned in daily to hear what the colorful yet fiery prophet would say next. His stuff was the talk of the town. More times than not his prophecies were loaded with bad news. But not always.

For forty years he had faithfully predicted God's judgment on apostate Judah. And, year after year, hostility mounted to his doom-filled messages. His temple privileges were revoked. His prophetic writings were seized and destroyed. Arrest warrants were issued. His zealous rivals sabotaged his work. He was abducted, publicly humiliated, tossed down a pit, and imprisoned.

More than once he wanted to resign the office of prophet, but God wouldn't let him. So he just kept doing the one thing he was born to do.

The inflammatory text that fueled his critics was always the same: *"Time is running out. Repent, for judgment is coming."* Jeremiah's repetitive warnings became the constant, rhythmic sound of God's clock winding down. *Tick...tick...tick...tick...* And every ticking moment haunted the Jews.

Few biblical orators have ever used imagery as effectively as the weeping prophet. Judah gasped when Jeremiah said, *"The Lord has covered Himself with a cloud so that your prayers will not pass through."* They cringed when he announced, *"You've eaten delicacies, but now you'll embrace only ash heaps."* They wept when they heard, *"The tongue of your infant will cling to the roof of its mouth for thirst. Judgment is near."*

Tick...tick...tick...tick...

And, sure enough—time *did* run out. Judgment arrived and Judah was carted off into captivity.

Unpopular messages have always been a staple with the prophets of God. And, not surprisingly, they're rarely the favorites among God's people. Repentance has never been what people want. But repentance has always been what people need.

Even the Lord lost audiences with unpopular messages. The John 6 crowd, miraculously fed, oohed and ahhed over His ability to cater a fish banquet from a kid's sack lunch. But the after-dinner conversation of "Eat My Flesh and Drink My Blood" was a real turn-off. Spiritual indigestion broke out everywhere.

Jesus' critics wrestled with two questions: "Why did He have to spoil a good meal with preaching like that?" And "How can I get another plate of fish...it's delicious!"

Tick...tick...tick...tick...

Even the Lord's disciples struggled with His unpopular approach. He asked them, "Does this offend you?" Their clumsy silence shouted, "Yes, as a matter of fact, it does!"

Tick...tick...tick...tick...

But unpopular messages don't have to be hopeless messages. Bad news is not always fatal news. Jeremiah, for instance, gave good news after Judah's thundering collapse. *"I have hope. The Lord's loving-kindness never ceases. His compassions never fail, for they are new every morning. Great is Thy faithfulness. Therefore I have hope in Him."* Even the most unpopular messages can have happy endings.

Strong medicine was never designed to taste good. It was designed to cure the patient. And as long as there's a pulse, we still have time for a recovery.

Tick...tick...tick...tick...

41

Letters From the Heart

—✺—

Letter writing is a lost art, and it's a real shame. Email, with its ease and speed, has become the *communiqué du jour*. But the email phenomenon will never duplicate the gritty character of good ol' written letters. Can email deliver the familiar scent of delicate perfume? Can email contain those annoying little sparkly things that spill into your lap? Does email allow you to emphatically pound the exclamation key so hard it bores a hole through the page? No! In short, email has no attitude. It can't strut.

Without fanfare, history was recorded through written letters. It was in a letter to Queen Isabella that Christopher Columbus first broke the news of the New World. It was in a letter to his colleagues that Galileo first revealed the secrets of his telescope. It was in a letter to his children that Louis Pasteur first exposed the medical marvel of inoculation. It was in a letter to President Franklin Roosevelt that pacifist Albert Einstein explained how to build, and why we needed, the atom bomb.

Letters often tell more about the writer than they do the subject. Leonardo da Vinci, perhaps the world's greatest artist, wrote to the Duke of Milan applying for his dream job—that of a soldier. William Randolph Hearst, the man who preached, "Never let the facts interfere with a good story," wrote his father with a strategy to make the *San Francisco Examiner* more profitable: "Let's hire naïve young men from the East who still believe there's fortune to be found in the West."

Sometimes letters even tell us what we *don't* want to know. Edgar Allan Poe, for example, wrote dark, pornographic love letters to women. On the other hand, Benjamin Franklin sounded like a total geek when he wrote of love. Their writings were true reflections of their souls.

WWII introduced V(ictory)-mail: a short one-page form that was fed into a photocopier, reduced to film, and carried to military bases around the world. The letters were then reproduced and delivered to lonely G.I.s. Unfortunately, the technology bogged down as heavy lipstick imprints on the V-mails kept jamming the photocopiers.

Flashback nineteen wide centuries: Letters, especially from the apostle Paul, the churches' chief correspondent, were the most talked about documents of their day. They were the *broadcasting system* of the early church. Each new delivery was read and reread by those who were eager to know more of their newfound faith. His letters became the church's sermon notes and Sunday school curriculum all rolled into one.

So closely was letter writing associated with the church, that Paul used this metaphor when he referred to the church at Corinth as his personal *"letter of endorsement."* Their changed lives validated his ministry. The proof was in their pudding. They were an example of what God's Word can do in a person's life.

It's a gutsy move to allow your congregation—as Paul did—to be *read* as a testament of your work, for your parishioners to be living presentations of your ministry, seen and studied for the life-changing effects that come from God's Word.

But Scripture is filled with living billboards whose lives took on a decidedly different tone when confronted with the *truth*.

- Matthew, once a tax collector but now an apostle.
- Mary Magdalene, once demon-possessed but now a follower of Christ.
- Nicodemus, once a ruler of the Jews but now caring for the crucified Savior.
- The woman at the well, once morally bankrupt but now an evangelist.

Each believer's life becomes a letter to the world, "known and read by all men...a letter of Christ...written not with ink but with the Spirit of the living God, not on tablets of stone, but on tablets of human hearts."

Each week you write another chapter in their lives. Write them well; they'll be remembered for eternity.

42

A Message Without Walls

—⁂—

What is it about the thirty-something crowd that seems to launch headlines?

For example, Martin Luther was thirty-four years old when he nailed his ninety-five theses to Wittenberg's door. Jonathan Edwards was thirty when his Northampton pulpit helped launch the Great Awakening. By age thirty-one, Charles Wesley had written many of his six thousand hymns including *And Can It Be That I Should Gain*. By age thirty-five Dwight L. Moody was considered the finest evangelist of the nineteenth century. And at age thirty-three Billy Graham founded his evangelistic association.

By age thirty most preachers have developed their gifts, even distilled their theology. They may have stepped through an open door or two. But some seem shot from a cannon, while most of us—even well beyond our thirties—labor in relative anonymity.

For us there's only a faint drum-roll and rarely any flashbulbs. Consequently, those who don't know better might think ours is a nine-to-five job, a backdoor delivery—blue-collar all the way.

But we knew that before we signed up. Our goal was never to hog the spotlight but rather to aim it on the One who deserves it.

That's all John Bunyan, a commoner from Bedford, England, wanted to do.

Bunyan was introduced to Christ through two books—the full extent of his wife's dowry. Those books, Arthur Dent's *Plain Man's Pathway to Heaven* and Lewis Bayly's *Practice of Piety*, opened his eyes to his sinful condition and stirred his insatiable desire to tell others about his Savior.

So at age thirty, Bunyan started preaching. But, as any seasoned pastor knows, preaching is never easy. And, because Bunyan lacked governmental approval to preach, he was picked up by the police, hauled off to jail, and tossed into a prison cell for the disgraceful act of preaching without a license. The nerve!

Finally, after three months of confinement, he was brought before the local magistrate and offered a full pardon on one condition: "Stop preaching the gospel!" But that was something John Bunyan couldn't do.

So back into the slammer he went—twelve more years of incarceration in the Bedford city jail.

He waived his chance at freedom because, more than freedom, preaching was an even greater gift. No conditional pardon could satisfy the heart that *must* proclaim God's Word.

But our God is never hemmed in by seemingly impenetrable walls. In fact, it was from that cell that Bunyan wrote *The Pilgrim's Progress*—next to the Bible the most widely read book in the world, serving as the No. 2 bestseller for centuries.

More than writing, John Bunyan had to preach. His small cell had one window through which he could see only the outer stone wall. And so each day Bunyan would do what came naturally—he would preach, through a barred window to any who could hear his voice.

Day in and day out, the unmistakable sound of the license-less preacher was heard through the streets of downtown Bedford. Passersby would stop their shopping to gather outside the prison wall to hear his message of hope. Bound souls looking for release would find Christ while kneeling beside the very symbol of their soul's imprisonment. Some preachers just can't be stopped—and neither can their message.

It must have been the same for the apostles in Acts 4 and 5. They were beaten within an inch of their lives, their integrity insulted, their livelihoods threatened, and their families intimidated. And yet, to hear them talk about it, they praised God for being worthy to suffer for Christ's sake.

That heritage is now ours. We're the twenty-first-century proclaimers, called of God to carry the baton for those who've faithfully served before us. It's our turn to preach the message of freedom, to bring the Good News to our world, and, if necessary, suffer for Christ's sake.

There may be no red carpet or splashy headlines highlighting your ministry, but don't be discouraged. Your reward is still to come.

43

Final Thoughts From the Mamertine Prison

—⫘—

With apologies to Jerusalem, and maybe Colorado Springs, the world's most intriguing Christian landscape may be ancient Rome and its northwest neighbor, the Vatican. In that small arena of antiquity sits an extraordinary example of religious contrast.

In one locale you'll be dazzled by St. Peter's Basilica, the famed Sistine Chapel, and the incomparable works of Michelangelo. Along with their Catholic equals they represent all that's big and glitzy about religion. And then, just down the street, opposite the Roman Forum, you'll be humbled by the lesser known and infrequently visited Mamertine Prison.

Nothing shows the stark reality of Christian ministry quite as clearly as this rarely visited dungeon.

The Mamertine Prison is nothing more than a glorified hole in the ground, yet it's believed to be the holding tank where Paul—as part of Nero's crackdown on Christians—spent the last days of his life. And while there Paul wrote some of his most important letters, including the two to young Timothy. The conditions were deplorable. The author's feet were bound. The damp, cold musty air was barely breathable. The iron grate covering the lone entry allowed dust-filled light as well as rain and cold to pour in.

And though Paul never complained about his inhumane conditions, the prison was the perfect setting to give his young plebe a dose of reality. There would be no sugarcoated ministry pill, no look on the positive side, and no enticing perks or bennies to sway the unsuspecting recruit to sign for the duration.

Timothy was probably in his early twenties when he sensed the tug to follow Paul and take up the mantle. But after shadowing Paul from city to city, he began to have second thoughts. The truth of Paul's ministry didn't match the slick travel brochure Timothy imagined. No one warned him about Paul's less-than-friendly ports o' call: his mentor had been lowered over the Damascus wall to escape a lynch mob; his teaching caused riots in Iconium, Berea, and Macedonia. Timothy must have swallowed hard as he watched the Lystra townspeople bury Paul under a pile of rocks, leaving him for dead. Paul was laughed at in Athens, called a fool in Corinth, brutalized in Thessalonica.

And when Paul wanted his protégé to carry on his work, it scared the socks off young Tim.

He must have wondered, "Is it too late to change my career path? If Paul, with all his credentials, was rejected, how will I ever survive this work? His testimony outshines mine. The whole world knows him. Only my mother and grandmother know me. This thing has disaster written all over it!"

Filling big shoes—or worse, big expectations—was Timothy's worst nightmare.

At some point every pastor has felt the same. We know those moments, the second guessing, the comparisons and fears:

- The sense of being in over your head.
- Knowing there's a faster gun at another church in town.
- Fearful of the next crisis within the congregation.
- Wondering if your sermons still have the zing they used to.
- Questioning if your ministry really makes a difference.

We've all wrestled these doubts at one point or another. Some take the easy route and look for a new church. But starting over can be a false reprieve. The dragons from one church have brothers who attend the next.

Paul's directive to Timothy was simple but straightforward: "Stir up the gift that's within you...God has not given us the spirit of fear but of love, power and a sound mind...don't be embarrassed by me or ashamed of the Lord, but be willing to suffer persecution if necessary…and hold on to truth!"

It's genuine wisdom. It's practical advice. It's our mandate.

Your current pastorate may lack the lure of greener grass, but the Mamertine Prison was devoid of glitter too. Yet few places on earth served as a more effective pulpit.

44

There's Gold in Those Seas

—〰—

Eureka! The gold rush is on—again!

It's been nearly 160 years since half a million minors from around the world brought their picks and shovels to Sutter's Mill in 1849 pre-statehood California. It was the country's biggest news, headlined on every front page, even announced by President James Polk in an address to Congress. And with each successive year another half-million joined the digging force. The mother-lode, bless her heart, had given birth to gold, lots and lots of gold.

Fast forward to 2007—the mother-lode has a sister. But instead of a pick and shovel to retrieve your fortune, you'll need a petri dish; instead of a pack mule, get scuba gear.

But I digress.

Just recently scientists discovered a world of unusual microscopic organisms known as *extremophiles* that serve as nature's recycle centers. These tiny living creatures literally breathe in dissolved metallic waste in the same way we take in oxygen. We breathe air but extremophiles breathe discarded minerals as their "oxygen." It's their daily bread, their breath of fresh air.

But even more astounding, when these organisms exhale, the once worthless matter comes out in its original solid form. In effect, the dissolved minerals are recreated into their original state. By breathing in and out, the extremophiles turn useless matter into useable material, as though it had been reborn.

As technology increased, enterprising scientists-turned-prospectors used this same procedure on the world's most valuable mineral—gold.

Deep in the ocean's underwater canyons, which house nature's most hidden hydrothermal vents—an environment known for spewing dissolved metals from the earth's hot core—are miles of deposits of dissolved gold.

And sure enough, when the extremophiles are introduced, the microbes rapidly convert the useless, dissolved gold into a solid and valuable metallic form. Now, the amount of gold retrieved from this process is small, to be sure. But make no mistake about it: It's gold—real, genuine, bonanza building, cash-cow producing, Fort Knox kindred, goose-that-laid-the-golden-egg *gold*.

What once was ruined and abandoned by the white hot pressure of this world has been made whole again.

Sounds ominously familiar doesn't it? It's what God—through our ministry—does every week.

Radically reforming His creation is God's specialty; giving new life to His people is His trademark. Throughout time, God's countless reclamation projects tell their stories loud and clear:

- Zaccheus had become a money-grubbing cheat among his own people. But one dinner with Jesus transformed Zaccheus into gold.
- Mary Magdalene, a temple of demonic insanity, had her curse cast aside by the miraculous power of Jesus, transforming Mary into gold.
- Nicodemus had devoted his life to the strict adherence of the Law and found himself bound by it. But one visit with Jesus transformed him into gold.
- A dejected Samaritan woman, suffering from shame and guilt, had an impromptu conversation with Jesus and was transformed into gold.
- Saul, who'd tormented the church and kicked "against the goads," had a one-on-one meeting with the Savior and was transformed into gold.

The story is always the same: what the world corrupts, God can fix. *"But God...even when we were dead...made us alive."*

Thankfully, there's a solution to the ruinous attraction of the world. *"You were continually straying, but now you've returned to the Shepherd."*

Even after our rebelliousness, our God can turn us into gold. *"He saved us, not on the basis of our deeds, but according to His mercy."*

And, amazingly, He uses the smallest of microorganisms as one more showcase of His transforming power. Even more amazingly, He's chosen us to tell His people all about it: His forgiveness, His salvation, and His transforming power.

No wonder people set their alarm clocks on Sunday morning. They don't want to miss what we have to say. We've got a message that's completely contrary to the world's.

Our God can transform us into pure gold!

45

Quickie Conversions—an Oxymoron

—⁓⁓—

His business card read: *Hemiunu, Pyramid Builder.*
In 2570 BC, armed with blueprints, surveyor's tools, and unlimited slave labor, Hemiunu rolled up his sleeves to fashion the world's most elaborate coffin for Khufu, Pharaoh of Egypt. In doing so he constructed one of the Seven Wonders of the Ancient World: the Great Pyramid of Giza.

Even then, pyramid construction was not your run-of-the-mill business. There were no mail-order kits to buy, no *Home Depot* for supplies, no *Pyramids 'R' Us* showrooms to visit.

Hemiunu's job was the equivalent of carving Mt. Rushmore with a butter knife or fitting the Eiffel Tower with pliers. And today no other manmade monument compares in size, detail, and sheer amazement.

This expertly designed rock pile celebrates the imagination of the dreamer as well as the aching back of the doer. The Great Pyramid stands 450 feet above the desert floor and covers 13 acres. It contains more than 2 million stone blocks, each averaging 2½ tons. And inside the pyramid's core are almost a quarter-mile of passageways, elaborate chambers, and several trap doors.

It's an architectural marvel, yet its massive complexity is built upon a very simple equation: (D x S + E + T = GP), or *Design multiplied by Substance plus Energy plus Time equals Great Pyramid.*

It's the same equation used in evangelism.

As with building a pyramid, bringing life to the human soul is never an instantaneous event. The words *quick* and *conversion* are mutually exclusive. The battle for the heart wouldn't stand for it. In fact, *quickie conversions* are code words for *"Don't you believe it!"* Instant believe-ism is most often filled with misunderstandings, deceptions, or both.

Redemption is also D x S + E + T, *Design multiplied by Substance plus Energy plus Time.* How many questions had Nicodemus asked himself before he brought his list to Jesus? How much heartbreak had the Samaritan woman felt before she gave her heart to the Savior? How many Christian testimonies had Saul silenced before he yielded to their message? How much bondage had the Philippian jailor experienced before he asked, "What must I do to be saved?"

A soul's conversion is a journey from 1 to 100. Each step is linked to another; no motion is wasted. It goes something like this:

- A man, invited to church, hears the gospel for the first time—1 to 6.
- He hears a friend's testimony—11 to 14.
- Curiosity causes him to read from God's Word—19 to 27.
- A co-worker shares the love of Christ—30 to 36.
- A Christian concert takes him from 41 to 45.
- He tunes in to hear teaching on Christian radio—47 to 54.
- He's back in church with an open mind—58 to 70.
- He asks a friend about your message—70 to 74.
- More Christian radio on a sleepless night—77 to 81.
- Someone walks him through the plan of salvation—84 to 90.
- He observes Christlikeness in a friend—93 to 98.
- He prays a prayer of faith and repentance—99 to 100.

The angels rejoice.

No word or action was wasted. Witnessing's accrual paid eternal dividends, all at the perfect moment. And the end result is the birth of a human soul—one of the *true* wonders of the world.

God's divine construction plan uses every message you give, every testimony shared, and every teaching program we air, "so that the body of Christ may be built up." There are no throwaway Sundays, no unimportant preaching times. Every time you stand before your people and proclaim "Thus says the Lord…" raises their notch of understanding and contributes to their walk with God.

Hemiunu has nothing on us. We're master builders too. Our tools are timeless. And what we're constructing will outlive the pyramids by an eternity.

Build away!

46

God's Stop Sign

—ɯ—

It's the stop sign in an otherwise productive day, the toughest assignment on our to-do list, the job we dread the most and save for last: "*Wait patiently on the Lord*."

We're soldiers! Prepping for battle, marching with comrades, attacking the enemy, and reclaiming lost ground is what we do. Khaki is our favorite color, battle fatigues our favorite suit. To sit and wait seems contrary to everything we believe and teach.

But there it is again, "*Wait on Me*."

"Wait for what, Lord? My engine is revving! Let's get going! I've got people to see, wisdom to dispense, lives to change. I'm built for action! C'mon Lord, let's get going!"

Yet time after time He says, "*Wait!*"

Now, before we take His not-in-a-hurry methods as a personal affront, remember He's the one who required Abraham to wait twenty-five years to fulfill a promise. He made Israel wait four hundred years for a deliverer, and Moses forty years to *be* that deliverer. God required a dumbfounded and confused Job to wait in pain. He made David wait during Saul's relentless eleven-year APB. He made Joseph wait in an Egyptian jail though he'd done nothing wrong.

Each unscheduled halt had its reason, though none of the participants knew it at the time.

Elijah was also told to wait. Scripture says he was from Tishbeh, a nondescript stretch of desert somewhere in "Gilead, east of the Jordan." Translation: *Nowheres-ville*. And from this obscure waiting room he was given an assignment—he was to square-off with Israel's horrible monarch, King Ahab. Elijah's wait had finally ended.

It may have been the prophet's first trip to the big city, certainly his first audience with a king. And, without protocol, offering no introductions or typical small talk, and showing no deference to Ahab's royalty, Elijah abruptly announced, "As the God of Israel lives, there will be neither dew nor rain for years, except by my word!"

Wow, what an opening! What a splash! If that's his opening act, what's next?

What was next was a long isolation. God sent the gutsy prophet back into hiding, along the brook Cherith—another locale no one had heard of. And in that lonely hiding place he was to drink from the brook, eat food airlifted in by birds, and ... wait.

"But for how long, Lord? We've got momentum on our side. People are finally talking about the things of God. We've got Ahab on his heels. We're front-page news. Let's not waste this opportunity. Let's strike while the iron is hot!"

Then came the voice, "I said, *wait!*"

For days and weeks, and maybe months, Elijah waited. And, because he'd turned off the water supply, the brook dried up.

Now the brook was gone, momentum was gone, and still he waited.

"Go to Zarephath," said the voice, "where I've commanded a widow to take care of you." And Elijah obeyed.

Whether it was waiting in the obscurity of Tishbeh, preaching in the spotlight of the king, waiting alongside a brook, or serving in the shadows of a widow, Elijah had been faithful. It's no wonder that God, at the prophet's word, sent fire from heaven to dazzle the Mt. Carmel crowd and forever establish Elijah as His man. He'd passed the test. He'd waited on the Lord.

Waiting on the Lord is a required course in ministry. And only those who pass the test can truly succeed.

- David passed—"I waited patiently for the Lord and He heard my cry."
- Solomon passed—"Wait for the Lord and He will deliver you."
- Isaiah passed—"Blessed are all those who wait on the Lord."
- Micah passed—"As for me, I will wait for God my Savior."

Waiting patiently on Him is a tough assignment because His timing is rarely ours. But it's still *the* assignment.

What do you say we move it up on the divine to-do list?

47

The Law of First Mention

—∿—

History is defined by origins—such as when George Washington said "So help me God" during his first inauguration, thereby setting precedent for every chief executive to follow. Or when "In God We Trust" was first stamped on a two-cent coin during the Civil War. Congress hoped it could reunite a fractured nation and redirect its heart toward the Lord. Some things just have staying power. Used once and *WHAM*. They're set in stone.

That's also true with biblical origins.

The Law of First Mention is the biblical method of studying a word's roots. By going to a word's origin you can sense the pulse of the word. It's like following a vein of gold to the mother-lode. Just as *first-born* and *first fruits* and *first day of the week* have significant meanings in Scripture, so do the first usages of specific words. It's the moment when mental light bulbs turn on.

From their first appearance in Scripture, words lead us through a verbal safari, each with its own story and lesson. For example:

- Although Adam and Eve were the world's first sinners, the word **sin** was first spoken by God in a warning to their son Cain—just hours before he murdered his brother Abel.
- The word **love** is first mentioned when God spoke to Abraham of sacrificing his son, Isaac—a foreshadowing of God's own sacrifice. Who could better understand Abraham's unfathomable grief than our heavenly Father, who would sacrifice His own Son.

- The word **salvation** was first directed to the tribe of Dan—a people who needed it most. They had popularized the sins of immorality and idolatry. And because they refused to repent, their name is later omitted from the tribes of Israel.
- The word **forgive** is first used in a lie.
- The first use of **grace** comes after sixty-five uses of **guilt**.
- As though capturing the entire Bible in a few chosen words, **righteous man** predates **wicked men**; and although **wicked** greatly outnumbers **godly,** the **King of Kings** arrives to throw **death's** last appearance into **the lake of fire,** as **righteousness** prevails in the end.

Bible stories within word-stories always have something to say. Just look at the first mention of *leadership* words in Scripture.

The word **encourage** first appears as Moses was handing over the leadership reins to Joshua. God told the older to "*encourage*" the younger. (I can't help but think of the famous Bellevue Baptist Church in Memphis, Tennessee. Adrian Rogers—now home with the Lord—had pastored Bellevue's 29,000 members for 32 years. Upon his retirement, Dr. Rogers installed the new pastor with a powerful display of encouragement by washing the younger's feet.)

Encouraging others is what we do.

The first use of the word **ministry** was in reference to those men who were assigned the task of carrying "the tent of meeting" during Israel's march toward the Promised Land. Each day, strong-armed faithful men would report to their assigned location, grab hold, and carry their portion of the Tabernacle. And to this day the word *ministry* continues to speak of carefully handling the work of God.

Heavy lifting is what we do.

The first use of the word **lead** was when God provided the unmistakable "*pillar of cloud by day and a pillar of fire by night*," so the children of Israel would never lose their way. And to this day biblical leadership is synonymous with ensuring His people are headed in the right direction.

Pointing the way is what we do.

There's much to learn from the Law of First Mention. And, most of all, we learn that things regarding His love, and our work, have never changed.

48

Christmas Wrapped in Questions

—〜〜—

Weary travelers had been strolling into Bethlehem all day, some from nearby Jerusalem, others from as far away as Nazareth, to comply with a political mandate to register for a new census. The whole idea seemed silly to some and disruptive to others—but it was the law, nonetheless.

Traveling in those days was a real grind. The rich had their camels, the upper-middle class had donkeys, but most folks walked. And since there were no travel agents, Auto Club maps, or advance reservations, a pilgrim ventured from home at his own risk—a *big* risk.

Navigating those rocky hills would challenge anyone. And the slower the traveler, the greater the odds of finding a *No Vacancy* sign hanging outside your favorite hotel. Woe to the slow-poke who got to town late.

By the time Joseph and Mary stepped into Bethlehem's city limits, the streets were deserted, every traveler tucked into bed. Even the crude shops that sold groceries, first aid kits, and baby supplies had long since hung a *Closed* sign on their door. Bethlehem's streets were rolled up, finished for the day. No one was outside—no one except a slow traveling couple, and she was full-term with her first child.

It's possible that some of the hotel guests heard the late arriving couple knocking on the door, first with knuckles and then harder with bare hands. The curious may have even peeked out a window to watch an exasperated Joseph beg the insensitive innkeeper for housing while Mary winced from sharp labor pains.

While counting his money the hotel clerk flailed a gesture toward the barn out back. And, with that, the weary couple followed the scent of the stable to their makeshift lodging, thankful for a place for Mary to lie down. It didn't matter that they were amidst animals, nor did barnyard conditions blur the moment. Because on that soiled floor the Savior of the world was born.

To those of us who've heard this story all our lives, it seems so plausible, so beautiful, even predictable.

But to those who had never heard, like those in Bethlehem, the entire story seemed surreal at best—or worse, absurd.

Joseph must have wondered, "Didn't the angel say this child was of God, and that He'd be a Savior? Then why did tonight turn out so badly? How can a Savior be born like this?"

Christmas has always been wrapped in questions.

Even when Gabriel first announced that Mary would "*be with child and give birth to a son,*" she flinched at the idea. It just didn't make sense. "*How can this be? I'm a virgin!*"

But God has always specialized in the extraordinary, and Christmas is living proof. Our Creator is outside any realm. He cannot be compartmentalized, nor does He conform to normalcy. He lives beyond limits. He is unrestrained by the impractical and laughs at the impossible. His understanding is infinite and His ways are immeasurable. He is, after all, God!

In nowhere else but Bethlehem was this more clearly demonstrated. Instead of being born in posh Jerusalem, Jesus was birthed in a nondescript suburb. Instead of attending royalty, He was visited by the working class breaking from their midnight sheep patrol. Instead of a royal cradle, He was placed in a feed trough. Instead of taking His rightful claim to the throne, He was rushed away to escape execution. *How can this be*? It didn't make sense.

But things rarely make sense in this world—whether it's His birthplace or our workplace.

Yet, as in Bethlehem, God is still in control. He doesn't follow our plumb line of expectations or reasoning—not on His Son's birthday, and not even today. He has His own plans. And, because He's the almighty God, that's enough!

49

The National Riddle Contest

—⟋ⁿⁿ⟍—

Buried deep in the apocryphal book of I Esdras is the story of three men handpicked by the king to compete in a National Riddle Contest. The riddle was: *What is the strongest thing in the world?*

A date was chosen and the town square reserved for the well publicized mental showdown. Each contestant prepped diligently, hoping to outwit his competitors. And each licked his chops at the thought of the great riches promised to the winner.

Finally the day of competition arrived. The first contestant smiled as he stood before the king and the overflow gathering. He spoke loudly and confidently. "Strong wine," he argued, "is the strongest force known to man. Its powers can control and confuse the best of men."

The audience applauded politely.

The second contestant waved off his competitor and proudly contended that he had found an even stronger force. "The king," he said, "is far greater than wine. He alone wields power among the nations. Kingdoms far and wide bow to his authority."

The crowd nodded their approval as they applauded, not wanting to insult the king.

Then a hush fell on the assembly as every eye locked onto the final contestant. They wondered, "How can he surpass the wisdom of the first two? What could be stronger than wine's influence or the king's great power?"

Walking slowly to the platform, the third contestant was fully aware of the enormous challenge. He bowed to the king, acknowledged his opponents, and then addressed the crowd: "There is one thing that surpasses the influence of wine and the power of our king," he said. "It is Truth. Truth is stronger than anything. Truth endures and lasts forever, long after the wine dissipates, and long after a king's rule ends. Truth lives on and prevails forever and ever."

The crowd stood and cheered.

Truth does indeed prevail. It has no expiration date, no time limit, no end at all. It's the only commodity in the universe that's as fresh today as it was in the beginning. And nothing in the future will change it.

Therefore, it's no surprise that Jesus would say to the Father, "Thy word is truth."

And, deep down, the world knows it. That's why, following the horrific events of September 11, 2001, sales of God's Word shot up dramatically and remained high for months. One estimate showed Bible sales up 25 percent worldwide just four months after 9/11. Though written thousands of years ago, the Bible has staying power. Our congregations—and our world—can't get enough of it.

Unforgettable characters, regardless of circumstances, have clung to that conclusion:

- Like Job who, in the midst of all his trials, said, "I have not denied the Holy One. I have treasured His words more than my necessary food."
- Or like Jeremiah, who bordered on depression as Jerusalem slowly slipped into idolatry and captivity: "I found Your words and I ate them, and they became the joy and delight of my heart."
- Or like the psalmist who, when contemplating the complexities of life, concluded, "The sum of thy word is truth. Every word you speak is timeless."

God's Word is sticky. That's why we labor in it, to study its depth, to uncover its riches, to declare its authenticity, to proclaim its authority, and to allow its power to impact lives.

Martin Luther thought like that. Often he said, "I study my Bible in the same way I gather apples. First, I shake the whole tree that the ripest may fall. Then I shake each limb, and when I have shaken each limb I shake every branch and every twig. Then I look under every leaf."

Some call ministry a job, but we know it's more, much more. It's a calling to "rightly divide the word of truth." Because *truth* matters.

50

Items of Inestimable Value

—⚭—

They've "starred" in Hollywood's biggest blockbusters. They cling to both the rich and the famous with casual ease. They're generally regarded for uniting people, but just as easily they've set nations at war. And though they're relatively small, they always gather a crowd. *They* are diamonds.

The world's love affair with these sparkly wonders began three thousand years ago. The ancients believed—because of the stone's ability to fracture light, and in some cases glow in the dark—that they were fragments of stars or teardrops from the gods.

Early kings would defiantly lead their troops into battle while wearing a diamond-studded breastplate, believing in their own invincibility because of the stones.

During the Dark Ages, diamonds were used to calm the mentally ill and to ward off demons. They were even believed to contain medicinal properties. Patients were told to hold a diamond in one hand while making the sign of the cross with the other. The wealthier patients swallowed the gems like aspirin as their *remedy du jour*.

Even the great minds were captured by the diamond's aura. Plato thought they were living beings. Other thinkers believed them to be male and female, claiming diamonds could marry and reproduce.

In 1477 Archduke Maximilian of Austria gave a diamond ring to Mary of Burgundy and thus introduced the engagement ring era. And, by placing it on her third finger of the left hand, he subscribed to the ultimate love theory—a belief that the *vena amoris* (the vein of love) runs directly from the heart to the tip of the third finger.

Whether it's the world's largest diamond—the Star of Africa weighing 530 carats—or a minute speck mounted on a bride's gold band, the diamond is considered the nearest thing to "priceless" that we can possess.

It's a nice thought, but it isn't so. If fact, according to the Bible, it isn't even close.

According to Scripture, there are still *four things* of greater value than a diamond, or for that matter a sea of diamonds, or a river of gold, or a mountain of silver. These four unfathomable valuables are:

1. **Wisdom**

   "…for it is more precious than jewels and nothing you desire compares with it."

2. **God's Ways**

   "…they are more desirable than gold, yes, than much fine gold."

3. **An Excellent Wife**

   "…for her worth is far above jewels."

4. **Personal Reputation**

   "A good name is to be more desired than great riches; favor is better than silver and gold."

And who would know better than the wise and wealthy men who penned these words—David and his super-rich son, Solomon.

The truth is, as beautiful and magnificent as diamonds are, they're still a simple chemical composition made of common carbon—like the graphite in a lead pencil.

But God's valuables are of inestimable worth.

For a pastor, much of every day is spent protecting these scriptural treasures, and with good reason. The enemies of God have deliberately and repeatedly tried to dilute, discredit, and destroy them all. The enemy knows their worth as well as God does.

And He, the maker of all diamonds, has yet to create one—or any number of pricy baubles—that can surpass the greatness of *His priceless four*.

In the constellation Centaurus, according to the Harvard-Smithsonian Center for Astrophysics, there's a white dwarf star that's been found to have a 1,864-mile-wide core of, yes, diamond. They've calculated its weight as 2.27 thousand trillion trillion tons. Or 10 billion trillion trillion carats—that's a 1 followed by 34 zeros.

What a rock! It's huge. But it's still just pure carbon.

Nothing compares to *God's incomparable four*. And we've been given the custodial duty to defend them all.

About the Author

—∞—

Ron Walters is Vice President for National Programming and Ministry Relations for Salem Communications, America's undisputed leader in providing and distributing Christian and family themed content via radio, internet, and publishing.

The company's far reaching ministry to pastors is unparalleled. Through the 50+ Pastors Events in 30 of America's largest cities, and the Pastors Letters, read by over 50,000 monthly, few pastors or churches have not been impacted one way or another.

Salem Communications believes that when God wins a city to Christ it's always through the local church and never a media organization. Salem believes the Bible teaching pastor of every community is the voice of God. Salem's role is never to replace or usurp the church but to serve as the platform for that community, raising the volume for those whose engaging and clear teaching of scripture should be heard.

That's why Walters has found a receptive audience with pastors and churches. He's one of them.

Pastoring a large California church uniquely prepared him for this ministry. And as a guest speaker in churches and conferences, he's learned the importance of teaching solid biblical content, the challenge of keeping an audience awake, and the wisdom to never sacrifice the one for the other.

Ron and Susan Walters (a business woman and writer) live in Santa Barbara, CA. Ron is a graduate of San Diego Christian College and did his post graduate work at Talbot Theological Seminary in Los Angeles. He's currently listed in Who's Who in Religion, Men of Achievement, and Personalities of America.

About Xulon Press

Have you written a Christian book? Are you looking for a Christian book publisher?

This book was published by Xulon Press, a part of Salem Communications. Xulon Press helps aspiring Christian writers get published. Founded in 1999, Xulon Press publishes more Christian books, title-for-title, than any other publisher in North America.

How can Xulon Press help you get published? We can turn your manuscript into a quality Christian book and get it into the hands of readers through 25,000 bookstores and on the Internet. You may purchase copies in any quantity, at any time. There is no minimum order and no obligation on your part to buy copies of your book. We make it a cinch and it takes only 90 days. With our unique publishing services, you will receive:

- A beautiful book cover design.
- Professionally formatted interior text.
- An ISBN for bookstore availability.
- Lightning-fast printing.
- Marketing and publicity.
- Author-friendly, no obligation contract.
- 100% royalty paid to you every quarter.
- Christian staff who will care about your book.

For a FREE publishing guide showing you how to publish your Christian book, visit www.xulonpress.com or call toll-free 866-381-2665.